seriously

business

Body Language

Using Nonverbal Communication
for Power and Success

SECOND EDITION

Jan Latiolais-Hargrave

KENDALL/HUNT PUBLISHING COMPANY
4050 Westmark Drive   Dubuque, Iowa 52002

ISBN 978-0-7575-4906-9

Dedication

To the Sisters who nurtured and educated me at Maltrait Memorial Catholic School, to my professors at the University of Louisiana who awakened my mind to learning and the power of knowledge and to my Cajun ancestry. These ingredients, in my "gumbo" of flavors, mark the magic that has helped me to treat others with the respect and dignity that I believe our Creator intended.

"There is hope for your future, says the Lord,
and your children shall come back
to their own country." (Jer. 31:17, RSV).

Contents

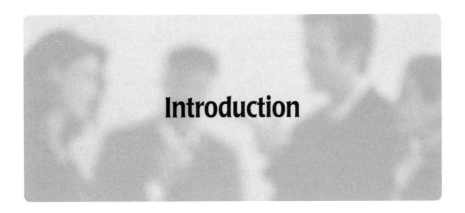

Introduction

The more times that leading newspapers, magazines, or television shows ask me to comment on an individual's body language, the more committed I become in my belief about the endless amount of information that one can gather from watching a person and reading his nonverbal communication. Politicians, Hollywood actors, and the regular guy in the street are all vying to find out what their bodies are communicating to the world around them.

Two amusing incidents happened several years ago that stand out in my mind concerning the accuracy of body language. The *New York Post* regularly contacted me for my opinion of people and their behavior at current events around the globe. During Bill Clinton's televised testimony, it wasn't unusual for them to contact me several times a week for my take on his body language. They asked, "Is he hiding something?" "Is he being truthful?" "What does it mean when he bites his lower lip?" "What about when he crooks his eyebrow?"

On one particular Friday afternoon, a *New York Post* reporter called and asked if I would take a look at three pictures and comment on each. She was writing a story on body language and was inquiring specifically about the placement of people's fingers and hands while seated. Of course I agreed, and I told the reporter to fax me the pictures immediately. She mentioned that she would not allow me to view the participant's faces, nor would I be able to see their feet. She further emphasized that she could not tell me if all three people sat in the same room.

From her urgency, I imagined that these were people who had interviewed for positions at the *New York Post*. I presumed she wanted confirmation about which of the three was the most reliable, most honest, and most suited for the job.

The first picture showed a man's hands quietly resting on his lap. His right hand cupped over his left; his thumbs intertwined together, and his little fingers twisted together. After studying his finger placement, I continued to examine the photo for more information. I noticed that he wore an appropriate business suit and a shirt that required cufflinks. Understanding the significance of cufflinks ignited further thoughts concerning the wearer's personality. A man who wears a shirt that requires cufflinks to a job interview gives a different impression than a man who interviews for a job and wears a shirt that simply needs a button. This clue reveals information about the position the person is seeking or it can indicate the degree of vanity in the man himself.

The woman's hands in the second picture sat comfortably placed on her lap. Her fingers lay widely spread apart with her right hand resting over her left. She wore a pinkie ring on her right little finger, had no wedding band, and wore a light colored suit. She did not have her legs crossed, and her feet seemed flat on the floor.

The third picture arrived quickly thereafter. It contained a woman's hands clasped together and held tightly in front of her, over her crossed knees. She was wearing a dark colored dress.

I recorded my findings and received the call from the *New York Post* reporter. She asked, "Do you have your analysis ready?" I said, "I certainly do!" She asked, "Well, what do you think about the guy?"

"Whoever this guy is, I would not trust him as far as I could throw him," I said. "I think that he has lied to you in the past, and I feel that he will deceive you in the future. In fact," I said, "I think that he's afraid of getting caught over something that he did. He's nervous, uptight, and holding back information." She said, "Wow, wait until I tell you who that is."

She then asked about the second person, the woman with her hands crossed on her lap. I told her, "She's the most honest of the three. She's prim, proper, extremely socially skilled, and knows what she's talking about. If I had to hire one of the three, you bet it would be this lady!" She said, "Wait until you find out who that is."

"What do you read from the third person's body language?" she asked. "She's seated in a courtship gesture," I answered. "A lady tends to cross her legs toward a man who interests her and away from a man who does not. She will then clasp her fingers together and hold onto her upper crossed leg, as she begins to feel more and more insecure. It is a gesture indicative of a woman who desires to hold onto the man she is with but who instead clutches herself in an effort to look 'prim and proper'." I continued by saying, "She's quite pensive and insecure."

The reporter cut me off and excitedly said, "Stop, I must tell you who these people are. You have hit the nail on the head." I said, "Who are these people?" She replied, "The first person is Marv Albert (the sports announcer), the first female is Barbara Walters, and the second woman is currently dating Marv Albert."

My second amusing story involves Starbucks Coffee Company and their search for someone to accept the role of 'strawologist' for them. Strawologist sounds confusing, doesn't it? Starbucks contacted me to introduce a new flavored drink and, as a special twist, analyze the body language and straw behavior of their coffee drinkers. I eagerly accepted the task and went about my research. I found that nearly 80 percent of straw users unknowingly provide silent clues about their thoughts simply by the way they treat their straws. Straw chewers enjoy attention and express themselves with animated words and emotions. Liquid-trappers and bubble-blowers are generally ostentatious and young in spirit. Multi-taskers use a multiple of straws, and people who are expressive and outgoing tend to use their straw as a spoon. Mavericks, those who refuse to use a straw, are unpredictable and unreliable.

In the last 20 years, and increasingly in the last 10, a great deal of research has occurred in nonverbal communication. This book summarizes many of the studies by the leading behavioral scientists and combines them with similar research done by people in other disciplines—sociology, linguistics, anthropology, education, psychiatry, family counseling, professional negotiating, and selling. The book also includes many features developed from the countless reels of videotape and film that I have reviewed, plus some of my experiences and encounters with the thousands of people I have interviewed, recruited, trained, and managed over the past 15 years.

To make it immediately as useful as possible, I have extracted 21 basic rules for successful silent speech. I explain these in relevant chapters and also collect them in the final chapter. If your primary concern is enhancing your silent speech sales skills as rapidly as possible, without concerning yourself about *how* and *why* each rule was formulated, then I suggest you turn straight to Chapter 13.

Silent speech is important to all of us. It significantly affects our chances of succeeding or failing in any encounter, whether personal or professional. Research suggests that the spoken words in any conversation contain only some 7 percent of the meaning. A complicated mixture of appearance, posture, gesture, gaze, and expression communicates the majority of information. This offers a potent instrument of persuasion to those able to use it effectively. It is especially important in situations where you suspect someone's attempts to conceal stress, disguise deceptions, or hide hostility.

The Contents describes the topics that you can expect to encounter in the book. Hopefully, these will help convince you that it will be worth your while to persevere reading the book and perhaps to participate in some of the practical exercises and experiments that each chapter suggests. My main wish, though, is that by the time you reach the end of the book, you will have a clearer idea of what is meant by the term *body language*, what types of behavior it includes, and what behavior it attempts to hide.

The entire book considers the role of body language in personal development, with discussion about its role in the area of negotiation, sales, and interactive skills. It examines how effective use of body language can contribute to personal growth and better performance during sales negotiations. In addition, the book explores the role of body language in the development of synergic relations, together with its role in establishing rapport, empathy, and a sense of togetherness.

This book's original purpose was to be a working manual for salespeople, sales managers, and executives, but any person, regardless of his vocation or position, can use it to obtain a better understanding of life's most complex event—a face-to-face encounter with another person.

Mastering the Nonverbal Art of Selling: A Framework for Understanding

Most individuals involved in sales and negotiations focus only on the verbal part of the encounter, yet during the average 30-minute sales call, buyer and seller exchange approximately 800 different nonverbal messages. Some negotiators make decisions based only on the tone of the speaker's voice, and some take each spoken word literally. Obviously, these are all necessary areas of interest. In the past, sales people who were aware of the importance of body language focused primarily on the voice and on facial expressions, but those are only part of the picture. The entire body—posture, gait, eye movements, gestures, feet, legs, torso, arms, hands, head, facial expressions and mannerisms—need analysis to get the true meaning of a message. These subtle messages conveyed without words reveal the buyer's true emotions.

History of body language

Since man's appearance on earth, he has communicated with body language. Babies easily "speak" to their parents through nonverbal communication. Even though parents sometimes accept the baby's message incorrectly, it is still a form of communication. Body language is a key to the inner psychological and emotional state of an individual. Not surprisingly, research indicates that the human body can produce over 7 million unique movements.

As far as the technical study of nonverbal communication goes, perhaps the most influential pre-twentieth-century work was that of Charles Darwin in 1872. His research generated the modern studies of facial expressions and body language. Current researchers around the globe have since validated Darwin's findings and observations. Dr. Albert Mehrabian, a noted researcher in the field of nonverbal communication, found that the total impact of a message is about

7 percent verbal (words only) and 38 percent vocal (including tone of voice, inflection, and other sounds), while a mammoth 55 percent comes through nonverbal expressions. Professor Ray Birdwhistell made similar conclusions about the amount of nonverbal communication that takes place among humans. He estimated that the average person actually speaks words for a total of ten or eleven minutes a day and that the standard sentence takes only about 2.5 seconds. Like Mehrabian, he found that the verbal component of a face-to-face conversation is less than 35 percent and that over 65 percent of communication occurs nonverbally.

Researchers in the field of body language generally agree that individuals use the verbal channel primarily for conveying information, while the nonverbal channel negotiates interpersonal attitudes and, in some cases, substitutes for verbal messages. Regardless of culture, words and movements occur together with such predictability that Birdwhistell concluded that a well-trained person should be able to tell what movement a man is making by simply listening to his voice.

Charlie Chaplin and many other silent movie actors, also pioneers of nonverbal communication skills, used this means to entertain and amuse many of us on the screen. Audiences classified each actor as good or bad depending upon the extent to which he could use gestures and other body signals to connect effectively.

Julius Fast published a summary of all nonverbal communication research done by behavioral scientists in a book in 1970. It was at that time that the public first became interested in and aware of the existence and importance of body language.

Understanding nonverbal communication is not only necessary for individual success, it is also a vital part of a successful sales or negotiation process. Since making selling easier and more rewarding is the goal of business, the sales industry recently decided on the value of understanding nonverbal communication selling power for increasing sales results, overcoming buyer resistance, and boosting overall sales profits.

Some sales people are still at level one in their understanding of nonverbal communication. Although most negotiators receive training and know how to say the right things, they often squander sales because of their negative nonverbal expressions and their failure to read buying signals in their customers.

three steps to increased nonverbal selling power

Reading a prospect's body language is not the only goal in mastering nonverbal communication. Understanding your own body language during the negotiation is of the utmost importance. Sales people usually gain expertise in this area in phases, with time and practice. As far back as 1985, Gerhard Gschwandtner informed the world of the three stages of awareness and skill that are necessary before one becomes an expert in verbal and nonverbal selling power.

Awareness of the Buyer

This stage involves learning the five major nonverbal communication channels and interpreting the buyer's nonverbal signals. It is a quick method for scanning the buyer for clusters of gestures. Instead of looking for specific movements or postures that indicate that the client is bored, defensive, or angry, a group of gestures from the five channels requires analysis. These groups of gestures can indicate whether a buyer is open and receptive to the presentation or whether there are obstacles to the strategy that warn the sales executive to exercise caution. They also can alert the negotiator to stop and redirect his sales approach entirely.

Awareness of Self

Your own nonverbal movements and expressions can make or break a sale. Ask yourself: "How can I communicate to display confidence in myself and in my product?" "How does the other person see me?" "How can I avoid communicating nervous, negative nonverbal signals during the call?" Constructive criticism from peers and videotaping yourself during mock sales situations will show you how you look and act when your mind is concentrating on what you are saying. Once you understand your own nonverbal behavior, and how you use it to interact with clients, you are more aware of your impact on others.

Management of Self and Buyer

Nonawareness, awareness, internalizing, and integration, the four behavioral concepts involved in the universal change process, are needed to reach the final stage of people reading. When reading nonverbal signals becomes second nature, you have fully internalized the concept of reading people. Awareness and examination of the prospect gives you the ability to:

- detect negative nonverbal signals early in the sale;
- respond faster and more accurately to the buyer's nonverbal signals;
- increase your ability in managing your own nonverbal expressions;
- intensify your skill combining verbal and nonverbal abilities.

Body language means communicating with the movement or position of the human body. It can be conscious or unconscious. Using nonverbal communication, clients are visually telling you when they are unsure, need additional information, want a chance to ask questions, or have strong objections. Your nonverbal responses can reveal if you are anxious or bored. If the buyer asks a question and you feel uncertain about how to answer, your body will convey your uncertainty.

The moment you meet the prospective client, he judges you by what he sees and feels. The process takes less than 10 seconds, but the impression is permanent. Whether you make or break a sale can literally depend on the silent signals that you send during this first contact. Being friendly and positive, reassuring and understanding, both verbally and nonverbally, allows you to exercise all 100 percent of your communications impact.

Inborn, genetic, or learned

Research and debate have discovered whether nonverbal signals are inborn, learned, genetically transferred, or acquired in some other way. Confirmation collected from observation of blind and/or deaf people who could not have learned nonverbal signals through the auditory or visual channels has occurred. Studying and scrutinizing the gestures and behavior of many different cultures around the world also aided in the findings.

Discoveries in this research indicate that some gestures fall into each category. For example, most children are born with the instantaneous ability to suck, indicating that this is either inborn or genetic. The smiling gestures of children born deaf and blind occur independently of learning or copying, which means that these must also be inborn gestures. When researchers studied the facial expressions of people from five widely different cultures, they found that each culture used the same basic facial gestures to show emotion. This led to the conclusion that emotional gestures must be inborn.

When crossing your arms on your chest, do you cross left over right or right over left? Most people are uncertain about which way they do this until they try it. If one way feels comfortable, the other feels completely wrong. Confirmation suggests that this may be a genetic gesture that cannot be changed.

We can conclude that basic nonverbal behavior is learned, some gestures are inborn, and the meaning of many movements and gestures culturally determined. Most basic communication gestures are the same all over the world. When people are happy they smile; when they are sad or angry they frown or grimace. Nodding the head is almost universally used to indicate "yes" or affirmation. It appears to be a form of head lowering and is probably an inborn gesture, as deaf and blind people also use it. Shaking the head from side to side to indicate "no" is also universal and may well be a gesture learned in infancy. The young child who has had enough to eat shakes his head from side to side to stop his parent's attempt to spoon feed him, and in this way he quickly learns to use the side-to-side head shaking gesture to show disagreement or a negative attitude.

ⓖesture clusters and similarities

One of the most serious mistakes a novice in body language can make is to interpret a solitary gesture in isolation from other gestures or other circumstances. Similar to any other language, body language consists of words, sentences, and punctuation. Each gesture is similar to a single word, and a word may have several different meanings. It is only when a word exists in a sentence with other words that an individual can fully understand its significance. Gestures come in sentences and invariably tell the truth about a person's feelings or attitudes. A 'perceptive' person is one who can read the nonverbal sentences and accurately match them against the person's verbal message.

Incongruence of gestures occurs when an audience observes a speaker standing behind a lectern with his arms tightly folded across his chest (defensive) and chin down (critical and hostile), while telling them how receptive and open he is to their ideas. A speaker who attempts to convince an audience of his warm, compassionate approach while running his hands through his hair or tugging at his left ear is typically unsuccessful. Sigmund Freud noted that while a patient was verbally expressing happiness with her marriage, she was unconsciously slipping her wedding ring on and off her finger. Freud was aware of the significance of the incongruence of gestures and was not surprised when marriage problems began to surface.

Observations of gesture clusters and congruence of the verbal and nonverbal channels are the keys to accurate interpretation of body language. In addition to looking for gesture clusters and congruence of speech and body movements, we should consider all gestures in the context in which they occur. If, for example, someone is sitting at a bus stop on a chilly winter day with his arms and his legs tightly crossed and with his chin down, it would most likely mean that he is cold, not defensive. If, however, a person uses these same gestures while seated in a negotiation, we could correctly interpret it as meaning that the person is negative or defensive about the situation.

ⓟhony body language

A commonly asked question is, "Is it possible to forge your own body language?" The general answer to this question is "no" because of the lack of congruence that is likely to occur in the use of the main gestures, the body's micro signals, and the spoken words. For example, direct eye contact is associated with honesty, but when the faker tells a lie, his micro gestures give him away. His pupils may contract, his nostrils might widen, or the corner of his mouth could twitch. These micro signals contradict the direct eye contact and the sincere smile resulting in a tendency in the receiver not to believe what he is hearing. Thankfully, the human mind seems to possess a fail-safe mechanism; a gut feeling informs the listener that he has just received a series of incongruent messages.

We use the face more often than any other part of the body to cover up lies. We use smiles, ear pulls, eye pulls, nose touches, and winks as attempts to cover up. The complication with lying is that our subconscious mind acts automatically and independently of our verbal lie, so our body language gives us away. A term describing this is "leakage." Since it is difficult to fake body language for a long period of time, the body eventually leaks out its true feelings and emotions. This is why people who rarely tell lies are easily caught, regardless of how convincing they may sound. The moment a person begins to lie, his body sends out contradictory signals. It is these signals that give us our feeling that the person is not telling the truth. During the lie, the subconscious mind sends out nervous energy that appears as a gesture that can contradict what the person has just said. People whose jobs involve lying, such as actors and poker players, have refined their body gestures to the point where it is difficult to see the lie. Thus onlookers believe their stories.

To deter us from spotting their lies, actors refine their gestures in one of two ways. First, they practice what 'feels' like the right gestures when they tell the lie. This is only successful when they have practiced telling the lie numerous times over long periods of time. Second, as difficult as it is to do, some liars (poker players) eliminate almost all of their gestures while they are relaying the lie or posing the bluff.

Psychologists have long known that some deception is a normal, healthy part of human behavior, often starting in children as young as five or six. In adulthood, most people lie routinely, usually harmlessly, throughout the day. Robert Feldman, a psychologist at the University of Massachusetts at Amherst, reveals that the average fib rate is three for every 10 minutes of conversation. Even when a liar consciously suppresses major body gestures, he still will transmit numerous micro gestures. These micro gestures include facial muscular twitching, expansion and contraction of pupils, sweating at the brow, flushing of the cheeks, increased rate of eye blinking, and numerous other microscopic gestures that signal deceit and occur within a split second. They are difficult to spot and usually only trained professional negotiators see them. Results show that the most successful interviewers and salespeople are those who have developed the automatic ability to read the micro gestures during their face-to-face encounters with other people.

To be able to lie successfully, a person almost has to have his body hidden or out of sight. Police interrogation involves placing the suspect on a chair in the open or placing him under lights with his body in full view of the questioner. With everything out in the open, the suspect's lies are much easier to see. Sitting behind a desk where the body is partially hidden helps to 'cover up' secret information. The easiest way to lie is through text messages, over the telephone, or on the Internet.

⑤ignals, cues, and symbols

Most people have felt the need to warn companions at a party that a dreaded character has just entered the room and is heading their way. In such a situation, the informer does not simply point or shout; he raises his eyebrows at his companions, jerks his head a bit in the direction of the dreaded person, and purses his lips to warn his conversation partner to be quiet. These signals, actions without words, are movements a person uses to communicate needs, desires, and feelings. Signals are a form of expressive communication.

A cue is a type of receptive communication used to let someone know what is expected of him. An adult might gently pull a child's arm upward by holding his wrist to cue the child to lift his arm during a dressing routine. A gentleman holds a woman's coat open to cue her that he is willing to help her put it on. A negotiator lets others know of his desire to speak by nodding his head three times.

Symbols are representative of an event, action, object, person, or place. Symbols are useful for both receptive and expressive communication. The American flag is a symbol that communicates freedom, integrity, and the spirit of a nation. A Rolls Royce automobile symbolizes an object that is quite expensive.

do you speak body language?

Most people are fluent in the dialect of body language because the sub-conscious mind is already an expert. Training to look for more nonver-bal messages involves trusting your intuition to make your impressions more accurate. A thorough understanding of body language allows an individual to be able to modify his own reactions and thus improve his negotiating skills. Try answering the following questions to determine your level of fluency in interpreting nonverbal communication.

1. Your friend has her hands on her hips. Is she feeling aggressive?

2. Making room next to you shows a new friend that she's welcome to join you.

3. Mirroring your boss's movements and laughing when he does shows him that the two of you have a good connection.

4. When interpreting body language, a person should form a conclusion after observing only one gesture.

5. If a person darts his eyes around the room, he is looking for an escape route.

6. Slightly touching a colleague's forearm lets him know that you find his story engaging.

7. When your client runs his hand through his hair, it signifies that he is nervous and wants to make a good impression.

8. Crossing your leg toward your client lets him know that you want to include him in your negotiation.

9. If your negotiating partner clasps his hands and holds them behind his head, he is conveying to you that he is in agreement.

10. Walking slower makes you appear more confident to others.

Close Encounters: Territories, Zones, and Awareness of the Five Major Channels of Communication

2

How closely a person positions himself to another person during a negotiation communicates what type of relationship exists between the two people. A prospect will quickly let the sales executive know his comfort level if he feels that the executive has invaded his space. He either uncomfortably shifts his position or simply backs away.

Close encounters

The amount of space a client needs to feel comfortable varies according to an assortment of factors. Cultural differences, age, sex, and personality all play a major part in the preferred style of negotiation. Generally speaking, Eastern Europeans, the French, and the Arabs prefer a much closer distance than British people do. Peers will tolerate a closer range of contact than people with a wide gap in age. Conversations between females will occur at closer range than male-female talks, and male-to-male encounters show the most distance. People who are outgoing by nature are comfortable in a closer, friendlier position than those who are shy or aloof. Once a prospect and a sales person have built a relationship, the speaking distance between the two decreases.

Because of these differences, estimates for the amount of space a person will need in a given situation vary. In a negotiation situation between a client and a sales person, the following ranges apply.

Intimate Space: Up to $1\frac{1}{2}$ feet. Back off. This is too close for business situations.

Personal Space: 1–2 feet. Use for longtime clients, and only if they are comfortable.

Social Space: 4–7 feet. This distance allows room for stretching and gesturing without invading the client's territory.

Public Space: 10 feet or more. This is a good distance for delivering a speech or making small presentations.

In the early 1960s, anthropologist Edward T. Hall coined the term 'proxemics.' Hall, one of the pioneers in the study of man's spatial needs, helped us to have a better understanding about territories and our relationships with fellow human beings.

A person feels that his territory is the area or space that he claims as his own. It includes the area that exists around his possessions. People view their homes, their cars, or even their special pews in the church as territorial possessions.

Along with his personal territory, man has his own private portable 'air bubble' that he carries around with him. The size of his portable bubble is dependent on the density of the population where he grew up. This culturally determined personal zone distance broadcasts to others whether the person is accustomed to crowding or prefers 'wide open spaces' where he can keep his distance from others.

ⓟractical applications of zone distances

While an individual will tolerate a person moving within his personal and social zones (2 to 7 feet), the intrusion of a stranger into his intimate zone ($1\frac{1}{2}$ feet) causes physiological changes to take place within his body. When an unexpected invasion occurs of a person's intimate space, the heart pumps faster, adrenaline pours into the bloodstream, blood pumps to the brain, and the muscles begin preparation for a possible fight or flight situation.

In other words, if a person puts his arm in a friendly way on or around someone he has just met, that person may feel negative toward the intruder, even though he may smile and appear to enjoy it so as not to offend. At the initiation of a negotiation use the golden rule 'keep your distance' to help others feel comfortable.

Attempt to judge a prospect's preferred distance by his seating arrangement. If he never moves from behind his desk, he is probably letting you know that he wants to keep his distance. If he walks over and shakes your hand, then he has just entered your 'personal space.' It is wise to move closer only if the client seems skeptical about what you are saying. The prospect may view other attempts to seem 'friendly' by moving closer as threatening. Unlike friendly negotiations, interrogations become successful when the interrogator sits or stands closer than the suspect prefers. A suspect will perceive uninvited severe crowding as threatening, such as when a policeman gradually moves his chair forward during an interrogation so that after some time the suspect's knee is between the policeman's knees.

To emphasize key points in negotiations, it is prudent that the sales person project sincerity and confidence by leaning slightly forward, maintaining eye contact, and using expressive gestures. The prospect may interpret leaning back and looking down as a lack of confidence.

The behavior of people entering offices reveals information about their believed status. Low status individuals tend to stay near the door upon entering. Those of higher status will approach the proprietor's desk. People of equal status will casually come in and sit down next to the owner's desk.

CULTURE, STATUS, COUNTRY, AND CITY FACTORS AFFECTING ZONE DISTANCES

The lack of awareness of the distance variation of the intimate zones for different countries can easily lead to misconceptions and inaccurate assumptions about one culture by another. Americans who meet and converse stand at an acceptable 2 to 4 feet from each other and remain standing in the same place while talking. A Japanese person feels comfortable conversing with another person in a smaller 10-inch intimate zone. Oftentimes when an American and a Japanese individual begin a conversation, it is as though they are slowly moving around the room. The American begins to move backwards away from the Japanese person, and the Japanese person gradually moves toward the American. In their attempt to adjust to a culturally comfortable distance from each other, they give the impression that both are ballroom dancing around the conference room with the Japanese person leading. When negotiating business, Asians and Americans might look upon each other with some suspicion, the Americans referring to the Asians as 'pushy' and 'familiar' and the Asians referring to the Americans as 'cold' and 'stand-offish.'

The amount of personal space required by an individual relates to the population density of the area in which he grew up. Those who grew up in rural, thinly populated areas require more personal space. People raised in crowded cities are comfortable with smaller space distances. Watching how far a person extends his arm to shake your hand can give you a clue as to whether he is from a busy city or from a remote countryside. Those who grew up in the city are comfortable with an intimate 18-inch 'bubble.' People brought up in a country town, where the population is far less dense, can have a territorial 'bubble' of up to 4 feet or more.

To shake hands a city person will step forward to greet his prospect. An individual accustomed to wide open spaces stands at a distance with his feet firmly planted on the ground then extends his hand forward as far as he can to meet the handshake.

When calling on a client inside his home, it is wise to ask where you should sit. It could be terribly offensive to sit in the head of the house's chair. The prospective buyer could become inadvertently agitated about this invasion of his territory and feel on the defensive.

Americans treat space similarly to the way they treat time. Seemingly, the larger the space demanded, the higher the status of the person demanding it. Americans who get moved to smaller offices, or who get crowded together, worry about their status in the organization. While window offices are high status in the United States, the Japanese expression 'he is sitting near the window' refers to an employee who has worked many years for a firm and sits near the exit, ready for his retirement.

The French are likely to place a supervisor at the center of a large room so that he is visible to all of his employees. With personal space and customs varying from country to country, it is clever to do research before international negotiations. In Japan everything is open and crowded. In Venezuela a person must quickly get comfortable with closer physical contact. In general, the following nationalities prefer a closer or more distant space on first meeting:

Preferred Distances	*Nationalities*
CLOSE	Arabs
	Japanese
	South Americans
	French
	Greeks
	Hispanics
	Italians
	Spaniards
MODERATE	British
	Swedish
	Swiss
	Germans
	Austrians
FAR	North Americans
	Australians
	New Zealanders

Other interesting observations concerning nonverbal communication space distances are readily evident. A person is often reluctant to pass between two people who are facing each other; therefore, those in conversation with others who do not want interruptions should simply face each other. To close off an interaction to intruders while seated, the parties should sit with their legs crossed toward each another. Couples who are exchanging confidences will often turn away from the general population in order to discourage other interactions.

People who are plotting together will approach each other from the side. It is as though they are literally 'positioning' up to a fellow conspirator. You can readily see this activity at political meetings and conferences. Women talking together will stand closer to each other than men who are talking to each other.

ⓔxploring the five channels

Since you are now aware of the important part spatial distances and nonverbal communication play in a sales situation, monitoring your client's body language may not be as complicated as it seems. After you have noted your client's special preferences, it is time to focus on his five nonverbal channels: body angle, face, arms, hands, and legs.

A quick scan of these five channels takes only seconds—a small amount of time to invest in the improvement of a sales career.

Gerhard Gschwandtner, international sales manager and training consultant, reported that "a client's body language is most reliable when it changes from one gesture or stance to another and the movement and intensity of these changes are the motions that give you answers in every sales situation." Eyes that constantly blink say something quite different from eyes that move from you to your brochures during the business meeting. Arms crossed casually, with a relaxed body posture, are not a cause for concern until they become more tightly crossed. If your client turns his whole body away from you, he's nonverbally telling you that he is ready to exit. It is always important to look for clusters of gestures in any of the five channels. A single gesture in one channel is the beginning of the sentence; several gestures grouped together complete the sentence and give the true definition of the message that the client is trying to convey. Scanning all five channels and using that information in a sales situation can immensely increase selling power.

CHANNEL ONE—BODY ANGLE

If the prospect is seated in an upright posture and all of his body movement is directed toward you, you are receiving a positive signal that the negotiation is heading in a successful direction. A client will sit closer to you if he feels comfortable and friendly; he will lean his body towards you if he is intent on listening to your presentation. Typically, the client is sending a negative message if he leans back in his chair.

During negotiations, it is wise to square your body and especially your shoulders toward your client. It is a way to let your prospect know that you are fully present in the conversation. You should avoid side-to-side motions because they suggest insecurity and doubt. Complete stillness or too much motion is likely to project nervousness or tension. Following is a list of some body behaviors and the message each communicates:

1. Slumped posture = low spirits, dejection
2. Erect posture = high spirits, energy, and confidence
3. Leaning forward = interest, openness, positive attitude toward other person
4. Leaning away = distrusting, defensive, and disinterested
5. Crossed arms = defensive, not listening, unsympathetic
6. Uncrossed arms = willingness to listen, accessible
7. Sitting on edge of chair = receptive, ready to listen
8. Unbuttoning suit coat = agreement is near

CHANNEL TWO—FACE

The face and eyes are the windows to the soul. We gain a great deal of information about a person's emotional state from the expression on his face.

eyebrow flash—This gesture appears almost universally at the beginning of the greeting phase. It is the rapid up and down movement of the eyebrows that signals acknowledgement of another person. It relays the pleasure one feels when he is in his acquaintance's presence.

eye contact—One can regard too much eye contact as communicating superiority or a lack of respect. The interpretation of too little eye contact is that someone is not paying attention, is covering up his true emotions, is being insincere, or is being impolite. If a client gazes past the negotiator or around the room he is probably bored. Direct eye contact signals honesty and interest; shifty-eyed people are typically hiding information.

facial expression—A person's state of health can affect facial expression. Anxiety causes a person's face to show stress. People who generally feel bad frown more than those who feel good. Depressed people smile wider and longer to cover up the fact that they are unhappy. Genuine facial expressions only last seconds. A quick flush or redness in someone's face gives out a clear warning that something is wrong. People even judge such things as criminality from the face; some believe that the more pleasant the face, the less likely it is that the person could commit a crime.

smiles—The smile is the most universally used and the most positive facial expression. Genuine smiles involve the whole face; the corners of the mouth turn upward and the eye corners crinkle. An unforced, confident smile signifies that the client is content with the information that he is hearing. Smiling makes us happy and has a direct, positive effect on all humans. In fact, research indicates that a person's expressions can directly influence his mood. Daniel McNeill, author of *The Face: A Natural History*, states that "though courtroom judges are equally likely to find smilers and nonsmilers guilty, they give smilers lighter penalties, a phenomena called the 'smile-leniency effect.'" Incidentally, clean, straight teeth are indicative of a person attempting to create a positive, reassuring first impression.

CHANNEL THREE—ARMS

Where a client places his arms, how he moves them, and the extent of his movements will give further information about his underlying attitude. In studying the arms channel, intensity is a key factor.

A defensive prospect raises his hands in a 'stop' gesture or has his upper arms and elbows as far back on his chair as they will go. The client who places one arm on the back of his own chair is displaying confidence. If the client feels negative about what he is hearing, he will lean farther away or go to a hands-behind-the-head position of dominance. When the client is leaning forward and has his arms well onto the desk, he is exhibiting interest in the proposal.

A client typically shows rejection to your ideas when he crosses or folds his arms across his chest. When he places his hands on his hips he is sending you a message of defiance and readiness to move on with the conversation.

CHANNEL FOUR—HANDS

Open and relaxed hands, especially when the palms are facing upward, are a positive selling signal. Tightly clinched fists represent defensiveness. People who use self-touching gestures, such as hands on chin, ear, nose, arm, or clothing, indicate that they are tense or nervous.

Watch out for hands and fingers that take on a life of their own. Fidgeting with hair, pens, paper, or paper clips are annoying and are all gestures typically done by those who are impatient or nervous.

CHANNEL FIVE—LEGS

A study of 2,000 people by Nierenberg and Calero in *How to Read a Person Like a Book* found that no sales occurred while the participants had their legs crossed. Even if the client appears to be open and positive, if he keeps his legs crossed he may have some minor hesitations that will prevent the negotiator from successfully completing the negotiation.

An individual who keeps his feet on his desk during a negotiation, displays an attitude of ownership, superiority, and dominance. Crossed legs or crossed ankles signal that there is something preventing a completely open mind. This seating position indicates that the client is feeling defensive or reserved and wants to be uncooperative. On the other hand, uncrossed legs send a message of cooperation, confidence, and friendly interest in the other person.

When the client crosses his legs away from the negotiator, he usually also shifts his body away, and the sales call is not going well. Although it is best not to cross your legs at all, a leg crossed toward the client is acceptable in the early phase of a sale. If the client mirrors the negotiator's legs-crossed-toward position, he is sending a message that he feels mentally tuned in to what he is hearing.

Clustering and consistency

A single gesture is similar to a word standing alone. Without a sentence to give it a context, one can never be sure of its meaning. Clusters of gestures are the sentences and paragraphs of body language. A puzzled facial expression shows only part of what the client is thinking. Does he need more information? Is there a point in the presentation that contradicts something he has heard from another company? Paying attention to the prospect's other nonverbal communication channels reveals a clearer indication of his feelings. If he feels puzzled and positive, the negotiator will want to act one way. If he feels puzzled and negative, the approach will go in another direction.

Increasing your nonverbal selling power

The goal for increasing nonverbal selling power lies in:

- ◉ Selecting the appropriate distance. Always allow enough space for the buyer to feel comfortable.

- ◉ Scanning the buyer's five nonverbal communication channels— body angle, face, arms, hands, legs—to read the correct message being sent.

the body language of failure—No eye contact, fidgeting, nervousness, defensiveness, confrontation, and poor posture. If apparent, a client will interpret these nonverbal messages as fear, weakness, or discontent. A negotiator should never mimic a buyer's negative signals; he should react to the prospect with positive, helpful nonverbal messages.

the body language of success—Good eye contact, a comfortable, erect body posture, and open gestures that move toward the buyer. These signals give the impression of power, confidence, and satisfaction.

Secrets to the Handshake: Palm Gestures

3

Throughout history people have associated the open palm with truth, honesty, allegiance, and submission. Oaths are repeated with the palm of the hand over the heart. When someone is being sworn in in a court of law, he holds the Bible in his left hand and holds his right palm up for the members of the court to view.

By using the handshake correctly during the first moment of physical contact with another person, an individual can confirm an already favorable impression or do much to correct an initially unfavorable one in less than five seconds. The handshake provides direct and immediate information about another person.

An experiment conducted to determine how people respond to a simple hand touch revealed that adults welcome contact. The setting was a college library. In one line, the library attendant brushed each student's hand 'accidentally' as he returned his library books. In the other line, the researchers did not permit the attendant to make physical contact with the students returning library books. Weeks after the experiment began the researchers noticed that the line of the library attendant who accidentally brushed the hand of the students was increasing daily. Even though the other line was shorter, the students waited in the long line to get the opportunity to return their books to the attendant who had made a connection with them. The results of this experiment dramatically underscore the importance of physical contact.

Handshaking is an ancient ritual. According to historian Charles Panati, folklore places the handshake before 2800 B.C. in Egypt. He speculates that because the right hand is the weapon hand, presenting it open and without a sword became seen as a sign of peace and acceptance. Although it seems ancient in origin, that same handshake is still the accepted form of greeting in our modern society. Both in social and business situations, the handshake is important.

A handshake conveys information six ways:

1. We look at the appearance of the hand: the length, shape, and cleanliness of the palm, fingers, and nails.
2. We sense the texture of the grip: whether the hand is soft and delicate or hard and rough.
3. We feel the degree of dryness or dampness.
4. We consider the amount of pressure used: ranging from overly strong to insufficiently firm.
5. We analyze the time spent in contact with the other person: increasing or decreasing the time spent shaking hands can significantly change the meaning of the handshake.
6. We judge the style of grip: the dominant style, the submissive style, and the double-hand grip each convey a different message.

Openness and honesty

Open-palm displays give hints as to whether a client is open and honest. When a person begins to open up and become truthful, he will open up his palms and his body toward the negotiator. This is a completely subconscious gesture accomplished without much thought.

Clients indicate relaxation and pleasure by appearing open and friendly. When the client leans forward, displays a genuine smile, and gives direct eye contact, he is indicating that he believes what he hears and probably wants to learn more. Bringing the right hand to the chest is a huge honesty gesture. It is similar to the gesture used when reciting the Pledge of Allegiance. In the Pledge gesture, the fingers are typically together; in the honesty gesture, the fingers are generously spread out.

It is possible for a person to make himself appear more believable by practicing open palm gestures when communicating with others. During a presentation, it is essential that a speaker use palm up, open-hand gestures that extend out and then come back toward him. It is as though the speaker is guiding the client into what he is saying. He should avoid crossing his arms during the entire negotiating process.

Signals of honesty and cooperation are:

1. Palms toward the other person, hand open
2. Lean forward in seat
3. Good eye contact
4. Uncrossed legs
5. Jacket open
6. Hand to chest
7. Feet flat on floor
8. Genuine smile

When a client crosses his arms across his chest during the negotiation, he is feeling defensive about what he is hearing. To alleviate this motion, you should place a brochure or a cup of coffee in his hand. Once he has to grasp the object, he must uncross his arms thus leaving him more receptive to what he is hearing. Research indicates that the more open the upper body is, the more open the mind is. Turning a chair around and straddling it, a common gesture taken by men, is negative and represents a shield between the speaker and the listener.

🅟alm power: dominant, submissive, and vertical handshakes

The hand is an intimate body part, yet we use it to convey outward personality messages. This one smallish moment forms an immediate connection with another person. The handshake's components could give the impression that it is a complicated task: a swift, elegant movement toward the waiting hand, wise use of the eyes, the grip strength, and rhythm. Wisely carried out, the handshake is powerful.

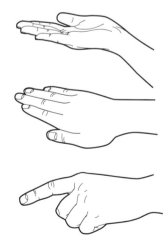

The four main palm command gestures are: the palm-up position, the palm-down position, the palm-closed-finger-pointed position, and the vertical position.

We view the palm facing up as a submissive, non-threatening gesture. It conveys a person's willingness to be subservient to another person's ideas. This is an appropriate handshake to use when attempting to help another person make a decision. The decision maker will get the impression of your willingness to listen and your ability to guide him in the proper direction.

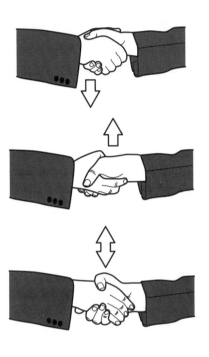

When the palm is turned to face downwards, immediate authority is achieved. The downward facing palm signals a 'take charge attitude.' The hand need not be precisely parallel to the ground to display this power handshake, but simply pointed downward in relation to the other person's hand.

The most effective handshake during negotiations is the vertical handshake. The hands touch web-to-web and typically pump up and down three times. This position reveals a message of equality between the two parties.

When a handshake features a pointed and extended index finger, the finger becomes a symbolic club that figuratively gives the message that the pointer "wants to have the final word."

ⓗandshake styles

Handshakes that we experience range from the "knuckle crusher" to the "dead fish." Ronna Archbold, writer and trainer in the field of protocol and sales, describes the five styles as follows:

1. **The "Knuckle Cruncher":** This type of person is earnest but nervous. Although he wants to convey warmth with his tight grip, he only succeeds in causing pain. The impression he creates is that of a person who lacks sensitivity. If he is wearing a ring, it can only aggravate the situation.
2. **The "Dead Fish Handshake":** Opposite of the "knuckle cruncher," this is when a person places a limp, lifeless hand in yours. This handshake sends a negative message; it is typically

indicative of a person who has a low level of self esteem. It can also be a sign of a person with a dreary personality.

3. **The "Pumper":** This handshake portrays a person who is overly eager but somewhat insincere. He does not know when to quit and seemingly stalls because he is not sure of his next action.

4. **The "Sanitary Handshaker":** This person barely puts three fingers in your hand and then withdraws them quickly. Such people appear timid, uncomfortable, and awkward.

5. **The "Condolence Handshaker":** This person could come across as too familiar at his first meeting with you. He clasps your right arm with his left hand as he shakes your hand. This type of handshake can work if the two people are familiar with each other, but on first meetings, it is too forward. The higher up the left hand is placed, the more familiar the two people are with each other.

Other handshakes common during negotiations are:

1. **The "Glove Handshake":** This is sometimes called the politician's handshake. In this style, both hands cover and submerge the other person's hand. When not sincerely done, it is a handshake that arouses serious doubt and suspicion. You should not use it at a first meeting, only after a warm relationship has already developed.

2. **The "Stiff-arm Thrust":** Aggressive types tend to use this handshake. Its main purpose is to keep another person at a distance and out of the initiator's intimate zone. Rural dwellers are comfortable with this handshake, but if a city dweller does it, it definitely is a message he is uncomfortable getting too close to you.

3. **The "Pulling the Receiver into Your Territory Movement":** This handshake indicates that the initiator is an insecure type who feels safe only within his own personal space.

4. **The "Tipsy Finger Handshake":** This handshake occurs when someone takes only your four fingers, doesn't allow you to really lock your hand with his, and then squeezes your hand hard. This can easily happen when someone is rushed or simply by accident. Wisely apologize and ask the person for a second handshake. It might seem awkward, but you do not want someone walking away from you thinking that you have not delivered a quality handshake.

Who reaches first?

The protocol for handshaking is simple to learn, but it does require refining. As you offer your hand to a person, simultaneously say with enthusiasm, "My name is . . . ." The person being greeted is often relieved and will usually respond by saying his or her own name. Studies reveal that those who show enthusiasm during the handshake are better liked, are hopeful and happy, and possess a high level of self-esteem. Word inflections accomplish voice enthusiasm. One of the most iconic scenes in American film is Robert De Niro in *Taxi Driver* as he practices a planned confrontation with another man. De Niro, as Travis Bickel, stands in front of a mirror and says, "You talkin' to me?" "You talkin' to me?" "You talkin' to me?"

Each time he says the phrase, he changes his inflection. But that is not all. He raises his eyebrows. He squints menacingly. He moves into the mirror. He leans back casually away from it. With each gesture, he conveys a slightly different message.

Thankfully, most of us will never encounter a psychotic character like Travis. But each day in our business and personal lives, we deal with people who tell us much more through their body language and voice inflection than the words they say.

It was once considered courteous for a man to wait for a woman to extend her hand, but that is not the case in business today. Either gender can initiate the handshake. It is also proper to rise to shake hands. Regardless of gender, rising to greet someone is a compliment; it shows liveliness and willingness to connect. Considering that the handshake is a sign of welcome, it is important to offer your hand first to your office visitor.

Meetings provide opportunities for "welcome" handshakes and "exit" handshakes. If the welcome handshake was not appropriate, it is imperative that the exit handshake be perfect.

Beverages should be held in the left hand at social events. This way you avoid the cold, damp feeling that the glass can give to your hand when you use it to shake hands with another person. Once an individual has mastered the handshake, it will become a normal part of his greeting. It will help to make a positive impression on everyone around.

Use the following guidelines to achieve a friendly handshake and to assess your client's attitudes and emotions early in your opening.

1. Start with eye contact and a smile. A great handshake is not just about a physical gesture, it is about connecting with the other person. It is a physical greeting that helps to convey pleasure in meeting another person.
2. Go for the web. Keep your hand open and make certain that your handshake will be a hand shake, not a finger or palm shake. This means getting the joint of your thumb nuzzled into the web of the other person's thumb.
3. Keep your hand in a vertical (straight up and down) position. Palm down communicates a dominant attitude; palm up communicates a submissive demeanor.
4. Apply moderate pressure—overly forceful handshakes (bone-crushers) convey aggression and a lack of consideration; limp handshakes (dead fish) convey insecurity or lack of interest.

5. Move your arm at a moderate pace—quick, jerky, overly enthusiastic hand pumping is too severe. No movement at all shows a lack of energy and uncooperativeness. Adjust the motion to what seems natural and comfortable to the other person.
6. Adjust duration. Some people prefer a long handshake; others prefer a much shorter one. Adjust the duration as to how well you know the person and what seems comfortable to him or her.
7. Pay attention to how your client returns your handshake. All of these interpretations apply to clients, too.
8. "Anchor" your message by slightly grasping your client's forearm with your left hand.
9. Close your handshake with direct eye contact and a genuine smile. Let the other person know that you were fully present during your short 'touching' conversation.

Your Price Is Too High:
Hand and Arm Gestures

What does your body communicate when your prospect says, "I can't pay that price." Think of your last sales call and try to remember specifics—your body angle, facial expressions, the position of your arms, hands, and legs. Most salespeople show negative changes in their body posture when hearing objections.

When a client sees signals such as crossed arms and legs, head scratching, swaying from side to side, nose rubbing, and shifty eyes, it intensifies your problems. The prospect may think: "Oh, I've found his weakness!" Even though your verbal reply is flawless, your nonverbal expressions may communicate "I'm feeling nervous" or "How will I convince you of the benefits of purchasing my product?"

Negotiators who communicate negative nonverbal signals after hearing the prospect's objections fail to recognize that negative body language gestures precede 99 percent of all customer objections. Positive gestures on the part of the salesperson are absolutely necessary, even if he does intermittently receive small negative gestures from his client. As soon as the salesperson notices the first disapproving nonverbal signal, he should manage and respond to it with open, concerned gestures in an effort to salvage the situation. It is far better to deal with slight rejections early in the negotiation.

What hand gestures reveal about thoughts

Evidence shows that people unsuspectingly produce gestures along with speech in any given communicative situation. These gestures elaborate upon and develop the content of accompanying speech, often giving clues to the underlying message of the speaker. Research also shows that gestures identify the deeper meanings to the words that a speaker does not or cannot articulate.

Body language experts note that hand gestures co-occur just slightly before hesitations, pauses, or a complex sentence. Individuals synchronize their gestures and words in time so that the 'stroke' (most energetic part of the gesture) occurs with or just before the most prominent syllable in the accompanying word. Typically the hand of a speaker comes to rest at the end of his speaking turn. Research in the area of nonverbal communication notes that 'gestural errors' are rarely made. A person's gestures practically never portray anything but his communicative intentions. A speaker may say "left" and mean "right," but he will almost certainly point toward the right. It is important to note that listeners take into account information conveyed by a gesture, even when the speech of the presenter does not reiterate this information.

Dr. Elena Nicoladis and her research colleagues observed the hand gestures of bilingual children as they told the same story twice, first in one language and then in the other. The researchers found that the children used a lot more gestures when telling the story in what they considered their stronger language. Based on the results of these and earlier studies, Dr. Nicoladis proved that there is a direct connection between language and memory access and gesturing.

If a person cannot find the right word during his negotiation, he might want to start moving his hands. Research at the University of Alberta suggests that gesturing while a person speaks improves his access to language.

The very act of moving hands around helps a person recall the words he needs to say; the gestures help access memory and language so that he can tell a more vivid story or recall important points to solidify his negotiation.

Since the left side of the brain (analytical, factual, numerical information) controls the right hand, and the right side of the brain (creative, intuitive, visual) controls the left hand, it is easy to understand how the movements of either hand can seek information from the appropriate side of the brain. When recalling facts, a speaker typically motions with his right hand. If the speaker is creating a story in his mind and sharing it with friends, he is highly likely to use many left-hand gestures.

Ancient studies label the left hand as the 'emotional hand.' Apparently there is an imaginary line that one can draw from the third finger of the left hand directly to the heart. Coincidentally, this is the wedding ring finger. People have named the right hand the 'proper hand' since they shake hands with this hand, take oaths, and use it to display honesty gestures.

ⓗand gestures

Rather than verbally saying "Trust me" or "I'm very confident about my presentation," an individual's subtle hand and arm actions can convey the message. The mannerisms of honest, confident people produce belief.

An open posture and a sincere facial expression should accompany open hands with visible palms. You should unfold, not cross, your arms and focus your eyes on the client. Shifty eyes suggest deceit. Generally, a person who looks to the left as he speaks suggests that he is recalling stored information and speaking the truth. Those who look to the right while speaking could be broadcasting dishonesty. An individual who looks down when he's speaking conveys to others that he is searching for an emotional response.

Not only is a large quantity of communication nonverbal, but the quality is high as well. Hands let the listener know that the speaker is changing topics. A dramatic movement of the hand or moving the hands wide apart easily signals factual importance. Basically, outward and upward movements of hands are positive actions. Downward and inward movements of hands represent control and self-absorption.

The hands-clenched position is visible when a person is frustrated or holding back a negative attitude. People who feel intimidated when being presented to a group also use it. The gesture has three main positions: hands clenched in front of the face, hands resting on a desk or on the lap when seated, and hands placed in front of the crotch when standing. The height at which a person clenches and holds his hands indicates the strength of his negative mood. The higher he holds his hands, the more difficult he is to handle. Since this is a negative gesture, some action is necessary to unlock the person's fingers to expose his palms and the front of his body, or

the hostile attitude will remain. In these cases, it would be wise for the salesperson to hand something to the client, a book or a pamphlet. As he picks up the object, his clenched hands will drop and he will become more open in his body language.

Covered hands, that is, resting the palm of one hand over the back of the other hand, is considered to be a barrier between two people. It is an act communicated by a person who is concealing feelings and covering insecurity.

HANDS STEEPLED TOGETHER

Putting the fingertips of one hand against the fingertips of the other is a form of 'steepling' that conveys confidence and superiority. A speaker uses it during presentations when he is self-assured about his information. Speech and drama instructors teach students to use this gesture to 'center' themselves when they are anxious about a presentation or when they have forgotten where they are in a lecture.

When a person is confident about what he is saying, he forms the steeple gesture at his chest level. When a person is confident with what he is listening to, he displays the steeple gesture at his lap level. If a speaker tilts his head back and then takes the raised-steeple position, he sends out a message that he is smug or arrogant.

The true definition of the steeple gesture, whether it is a negative or positive intention, is visible from the gestures that precede it. If a potential buyer uses a series of positive body language gestures (direct eye contact, body leaning forward), then places his hands in the steeple position, he is sending a message that he feels very confident about the ideas being presented. When this happens, the salesperson has received a cue to close the sale and should ask for agreement.

On the other hand, if the steeple gesture follows a series of negative gestures (arm folding, constantly looking at watch, head placed in his palm), the gesturer is signaling that he is confident he will decline the offer being presented to him. In both of these cases the steeple gesture means confidence; one has positive results and the other has negative results for the presenter. The movements that precede the steeple gesture are crucial to the accuracy of the gesture's interpretation.

CLINGING, TWISTED HANDS, FINGERS

Those who cling to objects during negotiations, such as notebooks, files, or tables, show a need for support. The action conveys confusion, insecurity, and difficulty in coping with the current situation.

Twisted hands (crossing both hands then clasping the palms together) are an expression of a complex personality or a difficult emotional life. This manner in which the hands are held together conveys a need to conceal information.

A person gives a message of anguish when he interlocks his fingers and his hands are rocking up and down with a wrist action. It is a position that imitates the bound wrists of a captive who is begging for mercy. A finger cross (where the middle finger of one hand is twisted around the forefinger of the same hand and the other fingers are held down) is a gesture that asks for protection. The phrase that often accompanies it is "I'm keeping my fingers crossed for you." If the gesturer wishes to protect himself (as when telling a lie), he may make the sign with his hand held out of sight of his companion. A variation of this gesture is called the 'hand fig.' It began as a child's game in which an adult reaches out to touch a child's nose, then pulls his hand away, showing the child his protruding thumb between his index finger and his middle finger, while reciting, "I've got you by the nose."

The forefinger point and beat during a negotiation is an authoritative gesture that indicates a moderate threat. The stiff forefinger portrays a miniature club where the speaker symbolically beats the companion over the head. A forefinger raise indicates that an individual wants someone else to pay attention to what he is saying. When a person breathes on his fingernails and then polishes them on his lapel, he is sending a message that he is thinking, "That was clever of me."

GRIPPING HANDS, ARMS, AND WRISTS

Prince Charles of the British Royal Family is noted for his habit of walking with his head up and chin thrust out while gripping one palm with the other palm behind his back. It is a superiority/confidence gesture position that allows the person doing it to express his vulnerable stomach, heart, and throat regions to others in a subconscious act of fearlessness.

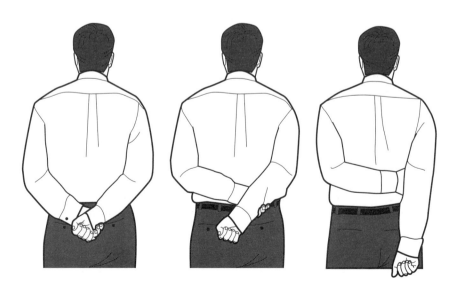

While the palm-in-palm-across-the-back gesture is a signal of confidence, we should note that the higher a person holds his arm behind his back, the angrier he is with what he is hearing. It is a gesture of frustration and attempt at self-control. The gesturer is saying, "I disagree with you so badly, but I'm holding myself back from punching you!"

THUMB DISPLAYS, HANDS TO LIPS

Thumb displays, in North America, are positive signals and are signs of proudness. Exposed thumps are used to display dominance, superiority, or even aggression. Visualize the executive sitting at his desk gripping his lapels and feeling intensely confident about his recent accomplishment. When a person places the tip of his bent forefinger upon his lips and keeps it there while he ponders, he is sending out a message that he either has something to say or that he would like the speaker to stop talking.

ⓗand parade

There are thousands of hand gestures, and each sends a message. Whether it is a chopping motion or an open-handed gesture, they all send visual signals directly to the right brain of the listener to augment the words that normally address the left brain. In reading clients a negotiator should look for:

1. Open and relaxed hands, especially when the palms are facing upward. These are positive selling signals.
2. Self-touching gestures, such as hands on chin, ear, nose, arm, or clothing, indicate tension. Probing for difficulties or simply relaxing the pace of the presentation can calm the client.
3. Gestures that contradict a facial expression. Actions speak louder than words, and these involuntary hand gestures indicate the client's true feelings. Watch for tightly clasped hands or fists that signal defensiveness.

Learn the messages that hands convey and use them to emphasize points: An open hand denotes honesty; a closed fist, aggression or evasion; a pointing finger, hostility.

Hear, Speak, and See No Evil: Hand-to-Face Gestures

How often would you guess you've been lied to in your life? Do you ever wonder if people are really interested in what you have to say? One way to uncover the truth during a person's conversation is to listen with your eyes as well as with your ears.

Recognizing nonverbal deceit gestures is the most important observation skill a person can acquire. People can tell stories, but their bodies tell the truth. There are two methods for deception: to *conceal* and to *falsify*. In concealing, the liar withholds some information without actually saying anything untrue. In falsifying, he takes an additional step: Not only does the liar withhold true information, but he also presents false information as if it were true.

When there is a choice about *how* to lie, liars usually prefer concealing to falsifying. There are many advantages to concealment lies. For one thing, concealing is easier than falsifying. There is no need to make anything up and no chance of getting caught without having the whole story worked out in advance.

Concealment lies are also easier to cover afterward if discovered. The liar does not go as far out on a limb and has many available excuses—ignorance, the intent to reveal later, or memory failure. The person who says "to the best of my recollection" provides an out if later faced with something he has concealed. If the truth later comes out, the deceiver can claim he did not lie about it but that it was just a memory problem.

❶ie detection

Adult nonverbal communication lying gestures stem from some childhood hand-to-face habits. If a young child tells a lie, he might cover his mouth with his hands in an attempt to stop the dishonest words from coming out. If he does not wish to hear his reprimanding parent, he simply covers his ears with his hands. He quickly covers his eyes with his hands or arms when he sees something that he should not. As a person grows older, his hand-to-face gestures become more refined and less obvious, but they still take place when he is covering up, perceiving doubt, or embellishing the truth.

If a person uses a hand-to-face gesture, it does not always guarantee that he is lying. It can, however, indicate that the person is uncomfortable either about the information that he is receiving or giving. Further observation of his other gesture clusters can confirm suspicions.

In most instances, the hand-to-face gestures associated with deceit occur with the left hand. This does not indicate that a left-handed individual lies more than a right-handed person. Reasoning for this rests in the fact that the right, creative side of the brain operates the left hand. Since a person's right brain activity associates with ingenuity and imagination, it is easier for words and thoughts stored there to come out or 'come to life' when the speaker uses his left hand. Further substantiation comes from the fact that throughout a person's life he learns to associate the left hand with bad or negative movements and connects the right hand with good or positive gestures. History shows that some countries so associate the left hand with negativity that they do not allow it placed on the dining table; they use it strictly for hygiene purposes. In any case, we associate nervous hand-to-face gestures, done with either hand, with a person's discomfort with his thoughts.

Besides hand-to-face gestures, researchers have noted that a variation in pitch frequency is one of the most consistently observed behavioral observations of deception. While lying, a person has a significantly elevated pitch frequency and a decreased rate of articulation. Researchers think that this increased frequency is the result of heightened physiological tension brought forth by the person's knowledge that he is not telling the truth. These speech disturbances appear directly related to an individual's mental process status. When speaking the truth, a consistent, repetitive, and almost rhythmic pattern characterizes a person's speech. When stressed, a person's speech pattern becomes slowed, inconsistent, broken, and contains increased speech errors. Occasionally, a deceiver's speech rate may dramatically increase along with an increase in speech errors. Even though a person tries to control his nonverbal behavior during deception, he is less successful at controlling his verbal behavior.

microexpressions

Microexpressions are 'brief and incomplete facial expressions that occur very quickly after exposure to a specific stimulus and before the individual can use active processes to conceal them.' These are difficult to self-monitor and almost impossible to restrain during deception.

These negative microexpressions can 'leak' briefly in a number of forms: unpleasant voice shifts, brief head shaking, nostrils flaring, nose wrinkling, and, most importantly, tiny facial twitching. Paul Ekman, author of *Telling Lies* (1992), provided empirical evidence supporting the effectiveness of microexpressions as a deception leakage clue. In his study he found that 90 percent of deceivers presented negative microexpressions during questioning, while only 30 percent of truth-tellers displayed any such behavior.

eye behavior

People typically state that they can tell if someone is being honest with them by looking into their eyes. Deception research provides evidence that this common belief holds true. Truthful, confident individuals focus directly at the listener during conversations. Any break in an individual's normal level of eye contact, if it occurs at an inappropriate time, is a potential sign of discomfort with what he is saying.

Excessive eye blinks and eyes that are closed for too long during conversations signal a person who is stressed or emotionally aroused. Consider both of these gestures as valuable body language leakage information during negotiations.

Research states that introverted liars show a dramatic decrease in eye contact, while extroverted deceivers show an increase in eye contact. Researchers believe the extroverted deceiver's eye reaction is due to his trying to challenge the interrogator or because he believes it increases his perceived sincerity.

smiling faces

At least 19 types of smiles exist. Those of most interest and value to the negotiator are the five basic smiles—those produced by the feelings of hollowness, pessimism, uncertainty, hostility, and pleasurable delight.

The hollow or oblong smile forms by wrapping the parted lips horizontally around the teeth. In other words, the corners of the mouth do not pull upward, but they simply stretch back toward the rear molars. This half-hearted smile is attractive, but it is a dishonest smile. It looks great, but it means nothing. In a genuine smile or laugh, the eye corners crinkle; with this one, the eyes remain more open. Genuine smiles involve the entire face, as the smiling person subconsciously uses the small muscles around his eyes to send out a message of happiness.

The smile of pessimism is indicated by a mouth that faintly turns down at the corners, similar to that of a half moon. People with this type of smile anticipate a dark, gloomy future and typically possess an unenthusiastic attitude. Although it is hard to consider it a smile, biting the lower lip or the lip-in gesture is one of the basic smiles because the upper teeth are bared. It is formed by making the upper smile and then tucking the lower lip in, between the teeth. This type of smile is indicative of a person who is in a state of doubt. When a person cannot make a decision, he bites his lower lip.

When feelings of hostility mix with efforts to be socially polite, strange smiles result. Severely forced smiles cause the eyes to squint, almost as though someone has squirted the person in the eyes with a grapefruit. A person who dislikes others but must pretend friendliness will display a grapefruit smile.

⒣and gestures that reveal thoughts

To ensure that an individual's hands will not give him away, non-truth tellers use them in a variety of ways. Such a person might tie his hands up in the activities of smoking, drinking, or clicking a pen. He may hide them in his pockets or he may even try to freeze his potentially revealing hands by locking his fingers together. A person typically brings his hands to his face so that he is aware of them, but once he places them there, he tends to forget about them. What a person does not realize is that the position of his hands on his face discloses his inner thoughts, feelings, and attitudes.

The hands-to-the-face gestures are an unusually rich source of information. Since the face contains four different sense organs, the specific organ that the hand goes to indicates whether the person wants to intensify what he is seeing, hearing, smelling, or saying.

When an individual places his hands in his pockets and keeps them there for an extended period of time, he sends a message that he feels dejected or depressed. If he begins to jingle the change in his pockets, it indicates the burden he is feeling concerning his financial condition.

THE MOUTH COVER

A person covers his mouth when he is speaking as a protection from letting the wrong words slip out. Deceitful individuals perform the mouth cover in a sneakier, more subtle way. The deceiver keeps his hand partially over his mouth and talks through his fingers. In this case, the hand is attempting to screen a fictitious answer or distract the listener from what is being said. As listeners watch people perform this gesture, they are often distracted by the

rings that the speaker wears, the watch that the speaker displays, or even the speaker's fingernails.

A person will place his fingers in his mouth when he is under pressure. While most hand-to-mouth gestures involve lying or deception, the fingers-in-mouth gesture is an outward manifestation of an inner need for reassurance. If a negotiator notices this gesture, it is wise that he furnish his client with reassurance and guidance.

When a person gets nervous, he tends to excessively lick his lips. His mouth becomes dry and his swallowing is strained, almost as though he is struggling to find the right words to say. Constantly clearing the throat is also a sign of nervousness.

THE NOSE TOUCH

If a deceptive person does not want to cover his mouth in an obvious manner, he will quickly brush the side of his nose with his finger. Again with this gesture, when the hand is over a part of the face it distracts the listener from the actual words being spoken. If a client rubs his nose or covers his mouth and is not speaking, it is an indication that he feels that the speaker is being dishonest with him.

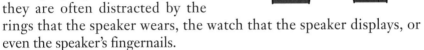

PINCHING THE BRIDGE OF THE NOSE

A person experiencing inner conflict and turmoil will often close or squint his eyes, lower his head, and pinch the bridge of his nose.

Closing the eyes serves to break contact from the conflict, and lowering the head shows the heaviness of the decision weighing on the individual's mind.

THE EYE AND EAR RUB

A person who places his finger over his closed eye and gently begins to rub is telling the listener, "Don't see very clearly what I am telling you, because I am lying to you!" The same is true with the ear rub, only this time the individual is telling the listener, "Don't hear very clearly what I am telling you, because I am lying to you!" A listener will also do these motions when he feels disharmony with what he is hearing and wants to relay a message that he has heard enough. Some people will conduct their eye rub by using a small, gentle rubbing motion just below the eye.

THE NECK GRAB

An individual who becomes unglued by a demeaning attack will often run his fingers though his hair and then grip the back of his neck. It is a response to mounting frustration. It is as though the person is trying to keep the blood that is rising up his neck from blowing the top of his head off. It is a gesture that starts off as a defense beating movement where a person raises his arm to beat an attacker with open hands, and then stops himself by placing his palm on the back of his own neck. He is giving the message that he feels the other person is a "pain in the neck."

When a person uses the index finger of his writing hand to scratch his neck just below his ear lobe, he is sending out a message of doubt and uncertainty. It is usually accomplished with five small scratches and is done so secretively that others seldom notice it.

THE COLLAR PULL

This gesture regularly happens when a person feels he is in a pressure cooker or on a hot seat. He feels 'hot under the collar.' It occurs as a person places his finger inside his collar then pulls the collar out and away from his neck, as if to let the steam escape. When someone reacts in this way, he is indicating that he is heated up and trying to defuse his own anger.

THE CHIN STROKE

A man will stroke his chin or beard when he is deep in thought and feels a desire to meditate over what he is hearing. Stroking, by its very nature, is a soothing action that implies easy thinking that is relatively free of conflict. Chin stroking is a nonjudgmental, reflective state of a listener; it lets a speaker know that the listener is appraising the facts that he hears. If you observe this gesture during a negotiation, look for the gestures that preceded it to determine whether it is a positive or negative chin stroke.

THE CHIN PUSH, THUMB POINT

The chin push is an indicator of strong opposition. It occurs by grabbing the chin intensely between the thumb and fingers with the thumb pointing up. The fingers curl down and around the chin and push upward. When a person is angry with what he is hearing, he grabs his chin in this way and pushes upward as if to keep from screaming. This gesture seemingly locks the jaws together and makes an outburst difficult.

THE CHIN REST, FINGER POINT

The chin rest, index-finger point is a gesture of genuine interest and evaluation. It is as though the listener is thinking, "How much of this information is true?" It is a positive gesture when negotiating because it informs the speaker that the listener is assimilating the information being presented. If the negotiator wants to have the listener stop analyzing the presented information and move on in his mind, he should place an object in the listener's hand to get the listener to change his analytical posture.

Variations of uncertainty gestures

A person who wears reading glasses will often remove them when he has to make a decision. He places one arm of the frame in his mouth indicating that he is uncertain as to how to answer a question. When an individual is asked for a decision and quickly places an object such as a pen, pencil, or paper clip in his mouth, he is signaling his hesitation about the answer he is ready to give.

In negotiating, the glasses-in-mouth gesture appears most frequently at the close of the discussion when a choice must be made. People who continually take off their glasses and clean the lenses are stalling for time. Temporary silence is the best tactic when observing this gesture.

The peering-over-glasses gesture is typical of a person who has a critical or judgmental personality. Whoever is on the receiving line of this look often feels as though he is being inspected or examined. People who wear reading glasses should remove them when speaking and put them back on to listen. This interesting tactic allows the wearer to have control of the negotiation while putting the other person at ease. The listener quickly learns that when the glasses are off, he must not interrupt the speaker, and when they are back on, he needs to start talking.

Pauses

Compared to those who are truly nervous, people who lie have longer pauses, shorter answers, and longer times between a question and a response. Liars need time to create their lies. When listening to a person's recalled experience, watch for stories that are too detailed and too chronically exact. Courtroom findings reveal that when a yarn is too chronically recited and sprinkled with an excess of unnecessary facts, it is typically a practiced tale.

anxiety gestures

Hand-to-face gesturers that a negotiator should avoid:

- Shredding napkins
- Playing with his hair
- Picking lint off of his clothes
- Doodling
- Making his hands into fists
- Sitting on his hands
- Holding an object and playing with it
- Twiddling his fingers or thumbs
- Holding his hands unnaturally still
- Shrugging his shoulders
- Putting his fingers in his mouth
- Biting his thumbnail
- Chewing on his lip
- Crossing his arms/legs
- Touching his face

Positive, Nervous, Negative, or Defensive: Arm Gestures

Common corporate photos often display people posing with their arms folded over their chests. This defensive stance can be traced back to the early years of portrait photography. Primitive cameras and chemistry forced 19th century portrait sitters to hold positions for a long time. To help posers keep still and remain calm, photographers positioned them with their arms folded.

Now, over 100 years later, people still assume this stuffy, stiff position on brochures or business cards. Because most people do not know what to do with their hands or arms, the easiest thing to do is to fold them.

Folded arms say plenty, for better or for worse, about a person. Such posing can express aloofness, hostility, strength, stubbornness, confidence, and arrogance. The folded-arms portrait of an executive in a white shirt on a dark background fails to express any significant aspect of the man's buoyant character. A woman realtor who poses for her business card with her arms across her chest is not conveying a caring, open message to prospective home buyers.

Studying and being aware of what a client's arms are doing gives clues to the prospect's personality. Generally, the more outgoing and open a person is, the more he will use his arms in big movements. The quieter and more reserved he is, the less motion he will exhibit. Since arms provide support for hand movements, their position gives an advanced warning of the hand signal that will likely follow. During negotiations, it is best to strike a natural balance between the two and to keep arm movements midway.

⑤houlder movement

Shoulders pushed back and straight are those of a person who feels good about himself and enjoys a high level of self esteem. Stressed shoulders are easy to recognize because they are a bit shrugged and make the wearer's head look slightly smaller. People do this when they lack interest or are feeling inferior. It is a gesture taken by someone having to take a crouching position when he is in a dangerous situation. When analyzing shoulder and arm positions, one should not confuse the raised shoulders of a frosty person with the lowered shoulders of an angry person.

When there is a difference in the level of shoulders (one raised, one lowered), it signifies that the listener doubts what he is hearing. With his uneven shoulders, the listener subconsciously indicates that he is weighing his possibilities.

In the shoulder shrug, the person hunches his shoulders up briefly and offers his hands in a palm-up position with the fingers spread. With the shoulder shrug, the person momentarily turns down the corners of his mouth and raises his eyebrows. This helplessness gesture is nearly always an expression of ignorance.

ⓑody blocks

People make attempts to shut out unwelcome messages by introducing a physical object between themselves and another person. It could be as simple a block as dark glasses, a newspaper, a purse, or folded arms across the chest.

Blocking is futher visible during stressful business negotiations when a distraught individual covers his eyes with one or both hands. When tense posture, a hostile expression, and little body movement accompany blocking, they often mark the end of an exchange. If, though, a relaxed body, a friendly expression, and some movement of the hands, arms, or body accompany the body block, then it serves more as a cautionary signal, and the negotiator should proceed with vigilance.

By folding one or both arms across the chest, the person forms a barrier in an attempt to block out the approaching threat, uninvited circumstances, or harsh words. Someone who feels threatened and has a nervous, negative, or defensive attitude will firmly fold his arms on his chest. This motion is also indicative of a listener who is beginning to tune out a speaker.

STANDARD ARM-CROSS GESTURE

In the standard arm-cross position, the person folds both arms together across the chest as an attempt to avoid an unfavorable situation. This universal gesture signifies the same distrustful or negative attitude almost everywhere. The typical message that accompanies an arm-cross gesture is, "I don't want to think like you think; therefore, I will put something between the two of us so that I do not receive your information."

The best approach for a negotiator to take when the standard arm-cross gesture appears from his client is to slow down and take a few nonverbal steps back. The negotiator has probably pressed too hard, and the other person feels insulted or fed up. A simple way of breaking any arm-cross body block is to hand the listener an object. Once the client accepts the brochure, cup of coffee, or folder, he has to uncross his arms. When his body language opens up, he has a tendency to be more accepting of what he hears. Research indicates that the more open a person's upper body is while he is listening to a speaker, the more receptive his mind is to accepting presented information.

STANDARD ARM-CROSS, FINGERS VISIBLE

The listener accomplishes this gesture when he crosses his arms but allows the fingers of one hand to be visible. Called the 'coach's position' or 'resting position,' it is the only allowable arm cross during negotiations. Arm crossing with no visible fingers is too defensive and negative to use during conversations.

FIST FOLD, ARM CROSS

This message is stronger and more intimidating than the standard arm-cross gesture. In this gesture, not only does the person cross his arms, but he also clinches his fists to signify that he is not merely defensive but highly aggressive. Since this is such a hostile gesture, a submissive palms-up approach is necessary to discover what caused the antagonistic feelings. Once a person assumes the fist-fold-arms-cross position, it is extremely difficult to regain the rapport that was initially created between the two negotiators.

Arm-Gripping Gesture

In this arm cross, the individual grips his upper arms with his hands so tightly that the blood seemingly drains from them, causing his fingers and knuckles to turn white.

This position represents extreme apprehension over a situation or great anger. Once a negotiator notices this type of fold, he should quickly realize that he will not be able to achieve any further progress. Wisely, he should turn the conversation around and allow the disgruntled client to express some of his concerns.

partial barriers

These types of arm crosses are less daunting than full-body blocks. They do not occur so much because someone is feeling negative about what he is hearing; they appear because a person is experiencing a lack of confidence. Partial barriers occur by placing only one arm across the body, by holding books or notebooks close to the chest, or when a person holds his own hand. A simple disguised arm cross occurs when a man swings one arm across his body to adjust his watch, cufflink, or shirt cuff on his opposite arm. These gestures are dead giveaways when examining nonverbal communication because they achieve no real purpose except to attempt to disguise nervousness.

other arm gestures

When a client rests his forearms slightly before him on the negotiating table, he is sending a message that he is ready for a quick retreat or that he wants to move closer. The negotiator should proceed cautiously. If the client pushes his chair back and places his arms and elbows as far back on the chair as they can possibly go, he is preparing himself to raise his hands and give the 'stop' gesture. These negative arm gestures give insight into the client's hostile attitude.

The prospect who hangs one arm over the back of his chair is communicating that the negotiator does not have his full attention. This position allows him to lean farther away from the negotiator and typically leads to the hands-behind-the-head position of dominance. The hands-behind-the-head position of superiority is too physically powerful for a two-person meeting. It conveys a message that says, "I think I am better than you are."

Clients who lean forward and place their arms well onto the negotiating table demonstrate their interest in the suggested proposal. Research proves that the more frequently the prospect handles the documents presented to him, the more likely it is that he will purchase or accept the ideas being presented. A client will typically use additional and extended arm movements when he is very intent on having his opinions heard.

When a person brushes his palms together (hands move up and down alternately, with the palms brushing against one another as they pass) to mimic the act of brushing dirt from his hands at the conclusion of a task, he is sending a message that indicates, "I'm washing my hands" of something or someone.

Positive body language to reassure the nervous client

The negotiator's arm gestures, shoulder actions, body blocks, position, stance, and movement during the conference can convey a sense of openness or defensiveness to clients depending on how he uses them. A negotiator should:

1. Avoid 'mirroring' the client's negative nonverbal gestures or movements. He should resist the subtle, subconscious urge to respond to these gestures by touching his own face, fiddling with a pen, jiggling coins in his pocket, or by shifting his posture too often.

2. Lead the client to imitate his own expressions of confidence and reassurance. He should communicate relaxed gestures and postures. The negotiator should maintain a comfortable distance between himself and his client and consciously lower his shoulders (raised ones indicate tension) and slightly tilt his head (shows interest).

3. Make broad hand and arm gestures. Tight, close-to-the-body gestures communicate that the negotiator is closed off to others. Broad gestures are nonverbal cues that encourage and invite others to participate in the negotiation.

4. Restrict arm folding. Folded arms communicate distance and create a barrier between the negotiator and another person. Though the negotiator may simply fold his arms in a relaxed way because he is comfortable, this gesture can distance him from others, no matter what the intention.

5. Limit hands-on-hips. Hands-on-hips can appear as a threatening and confrontational gesture. It is a readiness pose that relays to others that the negotiator is impatient and annoyed.

6. Stand still when stressing a point. Movement can upstage words. Too much movement can distract from what a person is saying and cause others to miss the point. When making an important point, the negotiator should stand still and establish a 'platform' for himself.

7. Use hand and arm gestures to give others visual clues about the presentation. When discussing numbers, a negotiator should illustrate what he is saying by using his fingers. He should use his hands when talking about visual images such as wide, tall, and short. These visual clues can lead listeners back to the discussion and the task at hand.

8. Use room arrangement to his advantage. To set the stage for a warm, informal discussion, a negotiator should move his chair from behind his desk. He should sit at the head of a rectangular conference table; it is the strongest leadership position.

9. Seat clients on his writing-hand side for cooperation. This arrangement makes it easier for the negotiator to get into the prospect's personal space. It also allows the negotiator extreme ease in pointing out information on documents that need examination.

10. Avoid finger-pointing. This gesture is traditionally a reprimand, an accusation, or a way of targeting a culprit. Instead, a negotiator should gesture to clients with an open, upturned palm.

Sales Hype or Selling Strategy: Leg Placement Tactics

Research shows that over half of all human communication takes place on the nonverbal level through body language. The position of a person's legs during negotiations needs further study. Any type of cross-leg position intimately reveals secrets to a client's thinking. In their study of 2,000 people, Nierenberg and Calero, authors of *How to Read a Person Like a Book* (1971), reveal that no sales occurred while participants had their legs crossed. Even if other parts of a prospect's body language (arms, hands, face, and body) are open and positive, if he crosses his legs he is indicating that he is experiencing slight uncertainties with regard to what he is hearing.

Since much negotiating time takes place sitting down, it is wise to develop and practice a confident, comfortable, and positive sitting position. A negotiator should begin by analyzing his motions when he walks into a room and sits down. What does he automatically do with his body? He should begin by scanning his five nonverbal channels to check for signals that might be damaging during a negotiation. Does he slouch in his chair? Does he lean forward in his chair? Does he rub his hands together? Does he tightly hold onto the arms of his chair? Does he cross his legs, constantly twist his feet, or straddle his chair? Negotiators strive to decode the prospect's gestures and body positions, but they rarely stop to think about their own gestures.

If a person's body language communicates earnestness, enthusiasm, and sincerity, people will tend to believe his message. If a person sends different verbal and nonverbal signals (conflicting messages), people will inevitably trust what they see and not what they hear. To be effective, the body language of a person's arms and legs must confirm and support his verbal language.

"**O**n my last leg"

Physically, human legs, along with feet, are the primary means of both support and motion. Symbolically they suggest mobility or stability. As such, the balancing of weight on the legs and the qualities of a stride are both legible as forms of nonverbal communication.

To 'stand on one's own two legs' is to take control or become independent. To 'be on one's last leg' or 'not have a leg to stand on' suggests failure or the loss of support and self-sufficiency. The value Western culture places on mobility renders legs symbolic of freedom and liberty.

The leg movements of the prospect give the negotiator an impression of how he is coming across. Observing negative signals can serve as an early warning to the negotiator. It allows him to correct his behavior before the irritation transfers to his client's consciousness.

When a person feels threatened his body language becomes defensive. He uses closure gestures and places the barriers of his arms and legs across and in front of him to defend himself from attack. When he closes himself, he substantially makes his body look smaller in an attempt to reduce the size of himself as a target.

are you getting comfortable?

The manner in which a person sits in a chair is not coincidental. If he is lounging with his arms and legs dangling, it is probably a sign that he is relaxed and feeling comfortable. If he is positioned on the edge of his chair with both feet on the floor, he is likely indicating that he is ready to leave. If he is seated with his legs stretched out in front of him, it is almost certain that he is signaling indifference. If a woman is seated back in her chair with her knees together, legs exactly parallel and feet in line, there is a strong indication that she is punctual, loyal, and meticulous. Although men and women sit quite differently during meetings, one can easily read attitudes and opinions from each position.

Like arm cross gestures, intersecting legs signal a negative or defensive attitude. Increased attention to the body language of legs helps an individual to decipher hidden feelings, prejudices, and suspicious intentions.

THE FIGURE FOUR LEG CROSS

The figure four leg cross occurs when a man places the ankle of one foot on the top of his opposite leg. Although men find this position comfortable, they should be aware that it signals a message to others that there is something halting them from fully accepting what they are hearing. When a client combines this masculine gesture with several upper body negative gestures, he is sending an enhanced message of opposition.

This aggressively masculine posture is offensive if used by visitors traveling to the Middle East because it involves the display of the sole of a shoe. Middle Easterners consider this action particularly insulting because they believe that the bottom of the shoe is the lowliest or dirtiest part of the body and dislike seeing it turned toward their faces.

THE EUROPEAN LEG CROSS OR FEMALE LEG CROSS

In this position, a person neatly crosses one leg over the other at the knee. It is the standard crossed-leg position of a woman, and is a position often used by males in European cultures. It can display an aloof or defensive attitude in a person, but in some situations the European leg cross simply indicates that the person is comfortable.

If a client switches to this position after the negotiator has presented several pertinent facts, the negotiator needs to change strategies. When the person combines this crossed-leg gesture with tightly crossed arms, he has completely withdrawn from the conversation. To break this seating position, a wise salesperson should ask probing questions to uncover the buyer's objection or increase the distance between himself and his client. When a woman sits in this position and slowly crosses and uncrosses her legs, she is subconsciously signaling that she finds someone attractive in her close proximity.

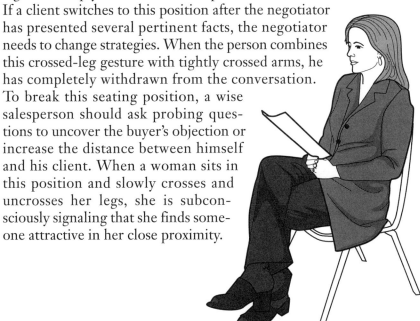

RELAXED ANKLE-ANKLE-CROSS

A male seated in this gesture loosely crosses his ankles and touches the floor with both feet. This type of ankle cross suggests relaxation because the posture makes it difficult to suddenly spring into action. The more dominant individual in a negotiation can afford to be in this state of less 'readiness.' This ankle cross is the least extreme form of leg crossing, and many consider it the most polite or most modest. It is the posture that sitting figures in a formal group photograph or statues of celebrated historical figures most often show.

HAND-LOCKED LEGS

In this cross, the hands draw the leg into the body and lock it there. In a negotiation, this gesture is evidence of a stubborn, highly-opinionated individual who is going to fight the negotiator every inch of the way. This clamp-like, extremely negative gesture signals an individual who may need a special approach to break through his resistance. It is a subconscious reaction of someone who is resisting persuasion in a discussion.

STANDING LEG-CROSS/ONE-ARM CROSS

These gestures occur when a person is standing and crosses one leg over the other or crosses one arm across his body. Labeled as partial body blocks, these gestures signal a person who is protecting himself from receiving information that he is hearing. It is a typical posture of someone who is being introduced to a group for the first time and is uncertain how to proceed with the conversation. Once the negotiator notices these gestures in his prospect, he should cleverly hand him something to read or to drink to get him to uncross his limbs and open up. Once he unlocks, the negotiator is in a better position to press home his point.

THE ANKLE-LOCK, FOOT-LOCK GESTURE

The male version of the ankle lock features crossed ankles with the feet pushed back under the chair. This seating position is usually combined with clenched fists resting on the knees or hands tightly gripping the arms of the chair. The female version varies slightly. In the female cross, the woman holds her knees together and slants her locked ankles to one side. In women, it is considered as the proper leg cross; in men, it is a sign of self-control and an willingness to share information with others.

No matter how relaxed the upper body may appear, generally speaking, the feet are the most honest parts of the body. In analyzing a client's body position, it is essential to note that the locked-ankle gesture represents someone who is holding back a negative attitude, emotion, or fear, even though his upper body appears receptive. When someone is feeling good and positive, his body will manifest what he feels. He gets happy feet. His feet begin to bounce up and down like a kid getting ready to be served ice cream.

Neirenberg and Calero (1971), leaders in the field of negotiating, found that whenever someone locked his ankles during a negotiation it meant that he was holding back a valuable concession. They found that, by using proper questioning techniques and positive nonverbal communication, a negotiator could often encourage the other party to unlock his ankles and reveal his hidden fears.

When analyzing leg crosses, take female fashion trends into consideration. Particularly notice how a woman's clothing might affect her leg positions before jumping to conclusions.

Other typical leg positions

feet on desk—This position indicates an attitude of ownership, superiority, and dominance. It is not a posture that will elicit cooperation from the client. Instead, it says "Go ahead and try to sell me."

legs crossed away from—This nonverbal gesture tells the negotiator that the sales call is not going well. When legs are in this position, the body also shifts away from the negotiator. Synchrony of thought is achieved when negotiating partners cross toward each other.

uncrossed, open—This is the ideal position for both the negotiator and the client. It sends a message of cooperation, confidence, and friendly interest. Feet should be placed flat on the floor to create an aura of stability.

legs crossed toward—To encourage a client to assume an open posture, this negotiating position is acceptable in the early phase of a sale. Once the client opens up, the negotiator should mirror only the positive gestures that he observes.

one leg entwined around the other—This position is indicative of a person who is imaginative and creative. If a client takes this position, the negotiator should be prepared to hear inventive solutions to objections. Because of the tight manner in which the coiler wraps his legs around one another, he gives the impression of someone who will thoroughly analyze a situation and who will be slow to unwind in the presence of others.

legs stretched out, one foot on the other—This position is indicative of a person who is confident but too relaxed for proper negotiating.

crossed legs at knees, with top leg slightly kicking—This is a gesture taken by a person who is ambitious, thoughtful, and planning a scheme. Clients who take this position during negotiations are plotting ways to win.

constant crossing and uncrossing of legs—This gesture is a sign of impatience and irritation in the listener. If the motion is calculated and slowly done by a female, it signifies that she wants to be noticed.

twisting the feet—This gesture is indicative a person who is extremely anxious and cannot keep his feet in one place. The constant foot movement is an outer expression of inner turmoil.

foot tap—The foot makes the movements of running away, but the body stays where it is. It is a conventional escape movement performed whenever the person concerned would rather be somewhere else but cannot, for social reasons, bring himself to depart.

crossed legs with highest foot in the direction of the speaker— This is a gesture that is indicative of a person who is relaxed, self-confident, and is listening with intensity.

how to size up the opponent (standing leg positions)

defensive and superior—Standing with locked ankles (holding back), thumbs out of pockets (superiority), and leaning slightly back (air of defiance).

defensive, negative—Standing with hand holding arm behind back (frustration).

defensive, aggressive—Standing with arms crossed over chest (defensive), back arched and chest out (defiance), one leg is slightly forward (aggressive).

defensive, anger—Standing with arms crossed over chest with hands tightly clenched (anger), legs are squarely planted on floor (firm negotiating position).

readiness—Standing with hands on hips in the British style with elbows pointed back (eagerness to negotiate).

authority—Standing with hands clasped behind back (authority, conviction).

mixed signal—Standing with one hand on hip (readiness) and the other hand in pants pocket (concealment).

buying signal—If the client gets up slowly and walks around, perhaps to look out of the window, he is evaluating or mulling over the opportunity before giving his final approval.

confidence—If the prospect stands with his hands gripping his lapels, he is confident with his own thoughts and decisions.

constant throat clearing and frequent coughing—These two gestures are indicative of someone who is nervous and hoping to cover up a lie. They are gestures that a speaker sometimes uses to help him to go on talking.

ⓑarriers to communication

A number of other barriers interfere with effective communication during negotiations. These factors do not influence the message as much as they prevent communication from occurring. They include: closed words, snap judgments, ranking, and inattentive listening.

Closed words are exclusionary words. Words such as 'all,' 'none,' 'everyone,' and 'never' are considered exclusionary words. They eliminate other possibilities and inhibit communication when used as part of generalizations. Not only would it be rare for statements containing these words to be true, but they typically prevent effective communication by evoking defensive responses.

Snap judgments, or premature closings, result when people make decisions based on first impressions or limited information. Those who make snap judgments based on appearance or on their first experience working with someone often extrapolate that behavior and continue to judge the other person the same way throughout the negotiating experience.

Ranking refers to a person's position or status. Conversational ranking is a barrier to communication when it prevents a person of one rank from talking openly to a person of another rank. It is common for a person of lower rank to be reluctant to report a problem to someone of higher rank. Also, communication problems can occur when a person of higher rank attempts a conversation with a lower ranking individual.

Negotiating partners must constantly look for chances to eliminate communication barriers. Since the word communication is derived from the Latin root word *communis*, a 'commonness' of understanding, interpreting a speaker's message means coming to a mutual understanding between the speaker and the listener. The focus during negotiations intensifies when individuals realize that there is a difference between hearing and listening (actively attending to information as its processing occurs). When unsure of a speaker's message, a negotiator should ask probing questions, paraphrase what he thinks he heard, and allow the speaker to understand that he has fully received his message.

Effective negotiators realize that they must get involved in discussions where the opposing partner totally reveals himself, his needs, his motives, and his desires. This is accomplished by asking questions, by noting mannerisms and context of speech, and by observing telltale gestures and other nonverbal communication.

Anatomy of an Encounter: Eye Signals and Other Popular Gestures and Actions

8

Have you ever wondered why some people seem to make friends easily, while others find it hard to form successful relationships with new people? The difference between those people who acquire new friends easily and those who do not is that socially successful people tend to make eye contact with their conversation partners much more frequently than those who are less triumphant socially.

Although the length of time that one person gazes at another is culturally determined, it is important to note that most North Americans want and enjoy an abundance of eye contact during negotiations. Some cultures possess such a high frequency of gawking that others may consider it offensive. Asians prefer to gaze at the neck rather than the face. Because of religious beliefs, Muslim women prefer that male negotiators look around them instead of directly into their eyes. North Americans refer to the client who does not make eye contact as "shifty-eyed" and regard him as someone who is untrustworthy. Understanding eye protocol, which is dependent on culture, is essential to successful communication. Whereas in one country a very intense, unblinking stare can make a conversation partner feel uncomfortable, in another country keeping eyes toward the ground signifies high respect for another person.

❸yes: the invisible grip

During the first year of life, infants learn rapidly that the looking behaviors of others convey significant information. Research indicates that babies prefer to look at smiling faces that engage them in a mutual gaze. Understanding this, it is easy to recognize why making eye contact is the most powerful mode of establishing a communicative line between humans.

Body language specialists have spent years preoccupied with the eye and its effect on human behavior. Phrases such as the "evil eye," "bedroom eyes," or the "sharpshooter eye," have been keenly used to describe eye behavior. These silent eye signals refer to the size of the person's pupils and to his gaze behavior. Eyes, labeled as "speech regulators," are the most revealing and accurate of all human communication gestures because they work independently of all other body parts.

Depending on illumination conditions, a person's pupils will dilate or contract as his attitude and mood change from positive to negative and vice versa. A person's pupils can dilate up to four times their normal size when he becomes excited or frightened. An angry or negative mood causes an individual's pupils to contract, making his "beady eyes" appear as though they have narrowed.

Since eyes, often labeled as the "windows to the soul," reveal concrete information about a person's interest level, it is wise not to hide them behind dark glasses during negotiations. These speech regulators seemingly give permission to another person to begin a conversation. Once eye contact occurs with another person, each individual scans the other's face for further information about attitudes and intentions based on silent eye signals.

History records that ancient Chinese gem traders watched the pupil dilation of their buyers when negotiating prices. If the pupils were large, it indicated that the trader was anxious to do business, perhaps too excited. The late Aristotle Onassis wore dark glasses when discussing business deals so that his eyes would not reveal his thoughts. Refusing to make eye contact can send a message of arrogance and contempt, and often communicates to the other person that he is insignificant and unimportant.

In North America we are taught to look people in the eye during conversations. In reality, a person seems to be able to make a deeper connection by looking at another person's pupils and acquire insight into his authentic feelings.

❶ook both ways before answering

In normal conversations, eye contact plays an important role as the regulator of turn taking. A person needs to first establish eye contact with someone to start a conversation; then, if the person looks back, he has granted permission to begin speaking. As two people enjoy a conversation, each looks away intermittently, then glances back toward the other to check in. When one conversation partner finishes speaking, he gives

First United Methodist Church
119 South Georgia Avenue
Mason City

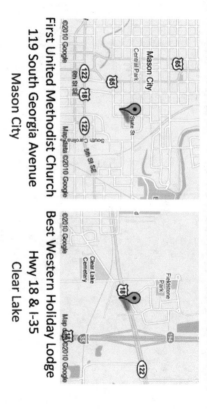

Best Western Holiday Lodge
Hwy 18 & I-35
Clear Lake

A block of rooms has been set aside at the Best Western for $69/night.
Please call 1-800-780-7234 or go online at www.bestwestern.com and ask for Latham/Bailey room block
Before September 30, 2010 to reserve your room.

The couple has chosen to not do a gift registry.
They ask that you might consider a monetary gift.

permission via eye contact for the other person to speak. If a person does not want to be interrupted, he should avoid the listener's gaze. Without eye contact, the listener will find it more difficult to interrupt, thus keeping the speaker in control of the conversation.

A listener looks at the speaker about 75 percent of the time in glances lasting 1–7 seconds in order to show his responsiveness and interest. If a person desires to make a verbal contribution, it is important that he reestablish eye contact with the speaker. It is more difficult in group discussions because a potential speaker has to give this signal to all of the others to let them know that he wants to speak. If the potential speaker feels he is ignored, he should make a shift in his position. This movement will steal the focus away from the present speaker. All eyes will then be on the person who wants to make a contribution to the discussion and he can proceed.

Where exactly does a person look while he speaks and listens? When pausing to select words, a person usually looks away from his audience and shifts his eyes to the left or to the right. In gathering his thoughts to answer a question, the hemispheres of a person's brain determine which way he looks. Generally, when seeking stored information, the eyes will go to the left. When seeking creative answers, eyes will travel to the right. Further, if a person is in conversation with someone who mumbles his words, he should lean in with his right ear in order to decipher the information with his left brain. If, on the other hand, a person is trying to identify a song playing softly in an elevator, he should turn his left ear toward the sound. The left ear is better at picking up music tones and sending them to the right, creative brain.

ⓖlances vs. gazes

Julius Fast, author of *Subtext* (1991), coined the term "moral looking time" when describing how long people should hold glances. In an elevator, on the street, or in an office building, it is appropriate to make contact, but a person who does not want to start a conversation should break it immediately. Any glance longer than a brief one becomes a sign of recognition or rudeness and can become a gaze.

The section of the person's face and body at which one directs his gaze is just as important as the length of the gaze during conversations. The differences between a business gaze and a social gaze can affect the outcome of a negotiation. An improper gaze can have a negative impact on the outcome of the meeting.

THE BUSINESS GAZE

Keeping a gaze directed at an inverted triangle on the other person's forehead (eye-eye-middle-of-forehead) allows a negotiator to create a serious atmosphere in a business conversation. He can easily maintain control of the interaction if his gaze does not drop below the level of the other person's eyes. It is a technique that allows the speaker and listener to leave the impression that each is attentive and committed to the conversation.

THE SOCIAL GAZE

Social gazing happens when the point of the triangle drops to include the chin area. This more intimate gaze allows the negotiator to look into the eyes of his client while also observing his mouth. It is a gaze that occurs in casual conversations between friends and allows the eyes to follow a natural, continuous path along the three points.

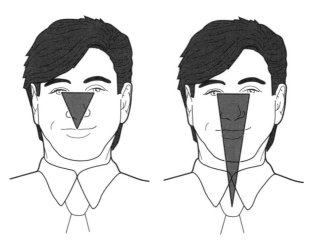

THE INTIMATE GAZE

This gaze goes across the eyes, below the chin, and down to the chest area. It is considered a very intimate gaze, and one should not use it in business conversations. If a person improperly looks "up and down" at another person he probably has a very personal encounter in mind.

Sideways glance and gaze aversion

The sideways glance, depending on what accompanies it, communicates either interest or resentment. Combined with slightly raised eyebrows or a smile, a sideways glance communicates interest. When the corners of the mouth turn down and the brows furrow, it signals a suspicious, aggressive, or disapproving viewpoint.

People interpret gaze aversion, which is looking down and to the side (usually to the right), to mean doubt, discomfort, anxiety, uneasiness, or guilt in situations of confrontation. During negotiations, a client who is ill at ease with the conversation will usually break eye contact and look down. Negotiators should be cautious of individuals who break eye contact too abruptly and shift their focus in ways that disrupt the atmosphere of professionalism.

Moderate eye contact is expected in all interactions. When someone temporarily breaks eye contact, it means that he is either processing what he is hearing or forming a response to a question. This brief interruption in eye contact shows that the listener is mentally paying attention to the negotiation, and the repeated return of his eyes to the speaker demonstrates his ongoing interest.

Eye-block gesture

Eye blocking occurs when a person keeps his eyes closed for longer than necessary or excessively blinks his eyes during a conversation. Both of these are irritating to a listener. They occur subconsciously when a speaker attempts to block out information that he does not want to reveal or wants to block another from his sight because he has become bored or uninterested in the conversation. The more threatened a person feels, the more frequently his eye blinks occur. The average rate of blinking for humans in lubricating the eyeball is about 12 times per minute. Therefore, a good measure of how much anxiety a listener is generating is to assess his numerous eye blinks. Falling asleep during a negotiation is the ultimate eye block.

A person who feels a cut above others uses the eye-block gesture while tilting his head backwards, universally known as 'looking down one's nose' at someone else. For effective communication to take place, a wise negotiator should change his approach once he notices this negative pose from his client.

Controlling a person's gaze

During a visual presentation using books, PowerPoint, charts, or graphs, it is imperative that the negotiator gain control of the client's visual gaze. Since 55 percent of the information relayed to another person comes via the eyes, using a pen or a pointer to point to the visual aid allows a negotiator to maintain maximum control of another person's eye direction. Lifting the pen from the visual aid and holding it between his eyes and the client's eyes makes the client lift his head to hear more clearly what the speaker is saying. This interaction allows the client to achieve maximum concentration of the presentation.

Using gaze with a large audience

When presenting to a large audience it is essential for a speaker to move his gaze so that each person receives some eye contact and feels included in the lecture. Excessive reading from scripts is a major drawback in providing eye contact; therefore, lecturers should try to memorize parts of their presentation. Ideal eye contact during a presentation is to directly gaze at one person for an entire thought or sentence, then move to another person and do the same thing. While directly gazing on one person, other people in close proximity also feel that the speaker is looking at them. This feeling of inclusion urges them to make a connection with the speaker. To avoid insecure moments, lecturers should focus on listeners who are smiling, nodding, and making eye contact with them. Positive audience members give the lecturer confidence and the energy he needs to continue. A presentation is not a one-way communication; it is a dialogue with an audience. Audience members may not be responding with words, but they are communicating with their eyes, their body language, and their facial expressions.

ⓣhe significance of wearing glasses

Attractive eye frames can create an impression of authority and intellect. They are ideal in situations where the negotiator wants to dominate or impress others with his knowledge. Negotiating partners should avoid tinted, dark, or reflecting lenses in business situations unless medically prescribed. Dark lenses tend to portray a person who is mysterious or detached. Eye contact during business dealings is essential to building trust with another person; therefore, eyes need to be visible.

ⓗead gestures: nod if you want me to continue

The two most widely used head movements are the head nod and the head shake. The head nod is an encouraging gesture used in most cultures to signify "yes," confirmation, or approval. Research shows that even people who are deaf and blind since birth use this gesture to signify affirmation. Used properly, head movements can help a person to communicate more easily. If misused they can quickly harm a relationship. Typically referred to as "speech markers," these head movements indicate a listener's attitude during an encounter.

People nod much more when they are listening than when they are speaking. Casual nodding is a major avenue used to show that a person is attentive to what another person is saying. Broadly speaking, the strength of the nod significantly increases as agreement intensifies. Rapidly nodding the head can leave the impression that a person is impatient and eager to add something to a conversation. Slower nodding, on the other hand, emphasizes interest, shows that the listener is validating the comments that he is hearing, and subtly encourages the speaker to continue.

When a person holds his head high and tilts it slightly backward, he is displaying intelligent interest. This head-up position is usually taken by someone who is analyzing what he is hearing. The head remains still but may occasionally give small nods.

Charles Darwin was the first to note that a human, as well as an animal, will tilt his head to one side when he becomes interested in something. The head tilt, accompanied by an eyebrow flash, often

occurs in greetings to achieve an extra degree of friendliness. When greeting, women use the head tilt, while men use the nodding gesture.

Slight head down positions signal an attitude that is negative or critical. Those who feel defeated in a negotiation or who disagree with what they are hearing often take this dejection stance. Women use this gesture to imitate submissiveness or a coy attitude. Therefore, unless one wants to appear humble or submissive, it is best to hold the head reasonably erect.

Though not recommended, people can even use head movements to beckon someone in circumstances where a shout or a wave would be inappropriate. This summoning movement takes the form of a diagonal throwing back of the head. It is typically repeated several times, depending on the urgency of the request.

hands clasped behind head

A person who is feeling confident, dominant, or superior will clasp his hands behind his head, nonverbally saying, "I think that I am better than you." Negotiators agree that it is far too superior a gesture to be done when only two people are in a conversation. In fact, most people find it to be annoying.

By enlarging his space intake, a person uses this gesture as a territorial sign to show that he has staked a claim to a particular area. It is a gesture used by a person who feels a need to run the show. Along with his hands clasped behind his head, a power person will feel the need to place his feet on his desk. This position indicates an attitude of ownership and dominance. It is not a posture that will elicit cooperation from a client. The hands-behind-the-head gesture creates the vision of an imaginary armchair in which a person lies back and tries to take charge of a situation.

ⓗand rubbing back of neck

A person will slowly and deliberately rub the back of his neck during times of frustration. Similar to a baseball player who rubs his neck after he strikes out and is walking back to the dug out, a negotiator will massage the back of his neck once he has reached an impasse. Accompanied by a tense face, the gesture implies that the client is not completely happy with the progress made thus far and does not quite know how to proceed. A wise negotiator should change strategies and proceed with more needs analysis questions if he observes this gesture.

ⓢtraddling a chair

Centuries ago men used shields to protect themselves from the spears and clubs of the enemy. Today, a person uses whatever he has at his disposal to symbolize this same protective behavior when he is under physical or verbal attack. This includes standing partially behind a doorway, sitting behind a desk, or straddling a chair. While straddling a chair, the back of the chair provides a shield to protect the body. Most chair straddlers slip into the straddle position unnoticed and quickly tune out what they are hearing. They are discreet and overbearing individuals who will try to take control of other people when they become disinterested in the conversation. This negative stance should not be used during negotiations.

ⓟicking imaginary lint

When a person disapproves of the opinions or attitudes of others but feels inhibited in giving his point of view, he performs displacement nonverbal gestures. Picking imaginary pieces of lint from his clothing is one such gesture. The lint picker usually looks away from the other people or toward the floor while performing this minor, irrelevant action. He is signaling disapproval. When the listener continually picks imaginary pieces of lint off his clothing it is a good indicator that he does not like what he hears, even though he may verbally agree with everything.

ⓐggressive and readiness gestures

The most common gesture used by a person to communicate an uncompromising attitude or decision is the hands-on-hips pose. It is a readiness gesture that carries with it an aggressive meaning. Labeled as the achiever stance, it describes the goal-directed individual who uses this position when he is ready to tackle an objection. People who are ready for action use this gesture to show an argumentative, dominant attitude. It is a strategy that a person uses to make himself appear larger and more threatening. A man will commonly use this gesture as a nonverbal challenge to other males who enter his territory.

An analysis of the gestures that appear immediately before the hands-on-hips gesture can help to make a correct assessment of the person's attitude. When the person takes this aggressive pose, is his coat open and pushed back onto the hips, or is it buttoned? Closed-coat readiness shows belligerent frustration, whereas when the coat is open and pushed back, it is an aggressive pose. The person is openly exposing his heart and throat in a nonverbal display of bravery. The individual further reinforces this position by placing his feet evenly apart on the ground to give the impression that he is taking a stand and will not budge. Women use the aggressive-readiness hands-on-hips cluster gestures to display critical evaluation and an impatient attitude.

Seated readiness

One of the most valuable gestures that a negotiator can learn to recognize is seated readiness. This occurs when the buyer places his hands on his upper thighs, casually leans forward, and places one foot slightly in front of the other. If a potential buyer were to take this position at the end of a sales presentation and the meeting had progressed successfully up to that point, the salesperson could ask for the order and expect to get it. Negotiators should respond to this positive signal with their own positive gestures. Since mutual positive gestures tend to reinforce each other, mirroring this gesture makes it easier for a discussion to proceed toward a successful close.

The starter's position

A person who leans forward in his chair and places both of his hands on both of his knees, or leans forward with both hands gripping his chair, is signaling a desire to end a conversation.

If either of these occur in the middle of a negotiation, it would be wise to terminate further discussion. Nonchalantly stopping the negotiation at this point allows a person to maintain a psychological advantage and to still manage later discussions.

ⓡocking/hugging

This gesture, made famous by Bill Gates, describes a person deep in thought during his conversation. The rocker grabs his forearms and begins a gentle rocking back and forth or soft swaying from side to side. Swaying is a positive gesture that stimulates pleasure centers linked to nurturing and encouragement and seemingly helps a speaker to analyze a situation. The embracing aspect of this gesture represents a portion of the development cycle that a person requires for complete actualization in his hierarchy of needs. Excessive rocking and hugging, though, are distractions to a listener.

ⓗere's looking at you

"Chin up, shoulders back," "Keep your distance," "Feet on the ground," "Pain in the neck," "Face me!" Body language emphasizes unspoken communication in every face-to-face encounter with others. A person can lighten the impression that he is making on another person by smiling more often, nodding, and by gazing at the entire face as well as the eyes, completely revealing that he wants to continue the conversation.

People Like People Like Themselves: Mirroring, Matching, and Building Rapport

9

Rapport is not a condition; it is a process of continually building a sense of trust and respect with another person. When a client feels that he is being heard and understood, he is comfortable about the communication experience. He trusts that the listener accepts his message. Insightful negotiators assume the responsibility for establishing and maintaining positive rapport. They know that by being "in harmony" with another's verbal language and body gestures, they can establish a climate that opens communication for a boundless flow of information.

Sitting back in a chair or sitting forward in a chair, using hands or keeping them still, putting an elbow on the table or keeping the elbows off the table, tilting the head or keeping it still, speaking faster or slower, raising or softening the tone of the voice, recognizing the client's preferred language—these are all types of physical mirroring and matching that are present during negotiations.

The key to establishing rapport is to obtain an ability to enter another person's world by assuming a similar state of mind. The first aspect to becoming more like another person is to match and mirror that person's behaviors. This synchronization serves as a powerful tool for getting an appreciation of how another person is experiencing life.

match your prospect's language

An individual can get clues about the type of information his client wants to hear by simply listening to his client's own choice of words. Since every person experiences his world through his senses—he sees, he hears, he feels, he smells, and he tastes—listening carefully to the language of the client is the most efficient way to determine language preference. By taking note of the client's representational system as expressed through his primary verbs, adjectives, and adverbs, a negotiator can ask

questions in the client's language. Using the client's words communicates to the unconscious mind that the two parties are "in sync." This sense of connectedness or rapport with another person feels as though the two are speaking the same language. Based on his preferred learning style, a person leans toward one of three major modes of language when communicating:

1. Visual-oriented language.
2. Auditory-oriented language.
3. Action-oriented language.

Wording that a person uses in his questions and answers inform the astute negotiator how to phrase his own statements and questions to get the client's attention.

visual—Prospects who prefer visual information will use phrases such as, "That's *clear,*" "I *see* what you mean," "Can you *show* that to me?," or "Can you *look* into that?" Charts, brochures, and actually viewing the product will gain the interest of these clients. During the needs analysis segment of the presentation, a negotiator should begin by using "seeing" phrases similar to the ones that his client uses. Once a negotiator recognizes the "visual" client, he should make a mental note of the areas of his talk that he can stress to make the most of his client's visual language preference.

auditory—Customers who prefer auditory information use sound words such as "That *rings* a bell," "That doesn't *sound* quite right," "Let me *hear* that again," or "It's as *clear* as a bell." Anything that makes noise will interest this type of client. He perks up when he hears the click of a new machine, the roaring of an engine, or the quiet hum of a fast computer. These clients attune more to the negotiator's tone of voice; therefore, concentrating on moderating volume and using a good range of pitch are necessary. "Sound" words used during the presentation are an absolute necessity.

action—Clients who desire action information use physical phrases such as "We'll have to *kick* that idea around," "I don't *grasp* what you are saying," "That doesn't *feel* right to me," or "I need to get a *handle* on this." These prospects prefer demonstrations where they can try out a product; they want to touch it, feel it, and even hold onto it. Presentations should include action words and anything that the client can grasp.

ⓜirror, match, negotiate

When people think alike, their gestures and body language tend to echo each other. Generally this is all subconscious. It becomes interesting when a person starts consciously controlling his movements. Some people find the idea of matching or mirroring another person's body motions uncomfortable or they see it as a way to take advantage of the other person. Realizing that matching and mirroring are a natural part of the rapport building process helps to overcome this uneasiness. People match and mirror gestures unconsciously each day with their families and close friends. Matching and mirroring done with integrity and respect create positive feelings and responses.

Mirroring and matching are powerful tools to smooth out negotiations, provided they get used appropriately. If the client catches what is going on, it will doom the negotiation. The best way to use the mirroring or matching technique is to always add at least one additional move between each mirror or match. If the client goes from crossed arms to placing his finger on the tip of his chin, the negotiator's motion would be to uncross his arms, perhaps jot something down with his pen and then mirror or match the client's position. A negotiator should avoid mirroring or matching throughout the entire session because the sophisticated client will recognize the technique and terminate the discussion.

Mirroring is a method of reflecting a person's behavior. To mirror a person who has raised his right hand, a negotiator would raise his left hand to form a mirror image of his client. The effect should be as though the client is looking into a mirror. To match this same person, a negotiator would raise his right hand; in other words, he would be doing exactly the same gesture (using the same hand, crossing the same foot, etc.) as the other person. Matching usually has a time difference that occurs between parties. If someone makes hand gestures while he is speaking, the listener would wait until it is his turn to speak before making similar (matching) hand gestures.

When a mannerism is idiosyncratic to a particular person, the negotiating partner should do crossover matching. If a client tends to repeatedly adjust his glasses and the negotiator does not wear any, he can simply move one part of his own body each time he observes his client's glasses adjustment. Skilled communicators typically possess a wide range of behaviors they can mirror to build rapport. For successful negotiations, it is wise to find a way to intermittently mirror virtually anything observable with a suggestive positive gesture. When the negotiator mirrors or matches elegantly, the other person does not become conscious of it.

To become proficient in matching or mirroring, a person can practice mirroring the micro-behaviors of people on television. Once he has become comfortable studying the behaviors of television personalities, he should try mirroring another person for a while. Once he senses that he and the other person are in rapport and are in a safe situation, he should scratch his nose or rub his eye. If his talking partner raises his hand to his own face, he can report that he has led the listener's behavior.

Mirroring another person's breathing pattern can help one to become in tune with that individual's mental and emotional state. When a person matches another's inhale and exhale rate, he can begin to feel the excitement or frustration that the client might be experiencing. Breathing in unison subconsciously helps to gain valuable understanding into another individual's state of mind.

MATCHING SELF-ESTEEM

The most convincing way to make a favorable impact on another person is to match that person's self-esteem level. When dealing with a group, it is best to match the self-esteem level of the most influential person present. If a negotiator's intent is to dominate another person, then he should present himself as more confident and more self-assured than his client. Self-esteem studies indicate that when people feel compelled to choose between low or high self-esteem partners, they are generally drawn to and select the latter.

BACKTRACKING

Backtracking or reciting back the information being heard, lets each communication partner know that the other understands him without judgment. It also allows for clearer understanding of the conversation. Backtracking is the thread that tightens and deepens rapport. It is repeating back the essence, not verbatim, of what the person is attempting to communicate. Being corrected during backtracking will only strengthen rapport because once a person backtracks the corrected information, the speaker really feels that he is being understood.

getting a word in edgeways

Even the humblest person can increase his chances of being listened to if he uses certain nonverbal behaviors. If a person wants to say something, of course he can simply interrupt. But there are more subtle methods. Speaking a little louder than the general level of conversation will often secure attention long enough for a person to make his point. Normal politeness will then enable him to lower his volume and finish. It is important, however, not to raise the volume by much because others may see this as rude and disturbing.

Normally a person will nod his head once or twice when listening. Making triple head nods, especially if accompanied by the words "yes," "but," or "well," works to let others know when a person is ready to speak. It signals something other than attention and agreement, and others interpret it as meaning that a person is ready to talk.

When a person raises his voice, it deters others from interrupting him. Again, though, others see it as rudeness if the increase in volume is excessive. A person can discourage interrupters by subtly keeping his hand in mid-gesture at the end of his sentences.

To help others get a word in edgeways, a speaker has several choices. He can simply come to the end of his sentence and pause or draw out the final syllable. He can also try ending his sentence with a prolonged rising or falling pitch or by simply looking steadily at the other person. If a person receives an opportunity to speak but wishes to decline, he can simply nod twice or request further clarification of the point. This encourages the speaker to proceed and allows him to further develop his presentation.

Studies conclude that listeners show increased synchrony of body movements at the beginning of the listening experience. They then settle back and show little movement at all until they notice that the speaker is coming to the end of what he is saying. At this point the listener begins to move quite conspicuously. This conspicuous movement signals that he now wishes to speak. Watching for and understanding these signals can provide a person with increased effectiveness in his conversations and discussions with others.

QUICK WAYS TO SHARPEN RAPPORT

A negotiator should:

- Take a genuine interest in getting to know what is important to the other person. He should start by trying to understand others rather than expecting them to understand him.
- Spot the key words or favorite phrases that someone uses and build them into his own conversation.
- Discern how someone likes to handle information. Does he like plenty of details or does he want to see the big picture?
- Implement gestures similar to that of the other person in terms of his body language, voice tone, and rate of speech.

body and foot pointing

The direction in which a person points his torso, or his feet, signals where he wants to go. A person shows agreement, interest, and receptiveness to others by turning his torso toward them. Angling the shoulders away indicates passivity, discomfort, or even dislike. When engaging in a conversation, a person sends an invitation to others to continue speaking by aiming his body to face theirs.

Foot positions also reflect private attitudes. A person who points his feet toward another person sends a message of inclusion; when he points them away, it shows that he would rather be somewhere else. Typically, a person will point his feet toward people he finds interesting and away from people that he does not like or does not find attractive. When a person decides to terminate a negotiation and wants to leave, he turns his body or swings his feet to point toward the nearest exit. Once he notices this body cue, the experienced negotiator would be wise to steer the conversation in another direction. Firmly planted feet indicate a person who wants to exhibit an impression of stability during the negotiation.

Inclusion and exclusion methods

During conversations, people typically stand with their bodies forming a 90-degree angle. This triangular stance functions as a nonverbal invitation for someone else to enter the conversation. When individuals engage in a private conversation, the body angle decreases from 90 degrees down to 0 degrees and the distance between the two people lessens. Both the open triangular position and the closed position, when used appropriately, serve as indicators for inclusion or exclusion of others by the initial talking partners.

When a third person wants to join two others who are standing in a closed formation, he receives an invitation to join the conversation only when the other two orient their torsos toward a mutual third point to form a triangle. If they do not accept the third person, the original two people in the conversation will hold the closed formation

position and turn only their heads toward the third person as a sign of recognition of his presence. Negatively, though, the direction of their torsos will show the third individual that they are not inviting him to remain.

❺eated-body formations

Two key angle seated formations can occur during negotiations: the open triangular position and the direct body point position. The open triangular position, where the individuals sit at a 90-degree angle from each other, lends itself to an informal, tranquil meeting. An individual can show nonverbal agreement with his associate from this position by matching his positive movements and gestures. As they do in the standing position, both torsos in the seated formation point to a third mutual spot to form a triangle that displays a shared agreement.

Turning a chair to point directly at a client nonverbally tells the client that the negotiator wants direct answers to his questions. Similar to an interrogation, when this seating arrangement is combined with the business gaze, the client will feel immense nonverbal pressure. The triangular seated position establishes rapport between two people; the direct body point is likely to create tension between two people.

open triangular position

direct body point position

to mirror or not to mirror

Mirroring and matching are methods of building a strong "second position" with someone else. They are fundamental behavior skills for modeling another person and for developing intuitions about a person's internal experience.

The following nonverbal cues are helpful to get a sense of the influence and effects of mirroring and matching.

Body hunched	➡	low confidence
Clenched fists	➡	aggression
Crossed arms	➡	shut off, uncomfortable
Dragging feet	➡	lethargy
Dropped shoulders	➡	weariness
Fidgeting with objects, hands	➡	nervous
Hands behind head	➡	arrogance, superiority
Hands on hips	➡	in defiance
Hands facing down on table	➡	in control
Head down	➡	timidity
Head resting on hand	➡	bored, disinterest
Leaning away	➡	disinterest
Leaning in closer	➡	interest
Looking at watch	➡	bored, impatient
Messaging temples	➡	anxiety, concentration, exhaustion
Nodding	➡	agreement, understanding
No eye contact	➡	lack of confidence, deceitful
Shaking of legs	➡	impatience
Shifty eyes	➡	nervousness
Tapping foot	➡	anxious, annoyance
Wiping hands on clothes	➡	uneasiness, edginess

Summary

Mirroring is not just useful for generating rapport; body language is a two-way street. The manner in which a negotiator carries himself, uses his facial expressions, and gestures with his hands gives others indications of his own mood. Once a negotiator has built up enough rapport with his client, that person will start to take cues from the negotiator's body language; in other words, he can influence his client's mood through his own posture, gestures, and expressions.

Communication connections are made by mirroring any observable micro-behavior:

- Body posture
- Spinal alignment
- Hand gestures
- Head tilt
- Blink rate
- Facial expression
- Energy level
- Breathing rate
- Voice qualities (volume, tonality, rhythm)
- Key words or phrases

Gender Communication Differences During Negotiations: What Did She Say?

Nothing is wrong with the fact that men and women negotiate differently or that they communicate in their own way. A problem arises only when men and women become insensitive to this difference. There are times when a person needs to adjust his negotiating approach depending on whether he is interacting with a man or a woman. The first step to creating equality in gender communication is to understand the different strengths and styles that each individual brings to the work table and to be aware of the different processes that men and women favor for decision making and leadership.

During negotiations, women tend to demonstrate an approach referred to as a "connectional" negotiating style, while the inclination of men is to adopt a "competitive" style. In rare cases, some men favor the former and some women favor the latter. A woman's nonverbal behavior during negotiations primarily aims at making personal connections, while a man's nonverbal communication style tends to parallel behaviors associated with dominance and power. A person's preferred negotiating style will quickly become evident during discussions. Wise negotiators who quickly recognize an individual's preferred style are in a better position to determine how to best influence his negotiating partner.

Where does gender behavior originate? Male and female conditioning starts with parents and parenting. Boys get handled more physically; they learn to be tough. They get picked up, bounced around, and tickled more than girls. Girls tend to get kissed, hugged, and patted more. As children grow, parents continue to socialize them differently. A child observes his father as he uses command terms during family interactions yet hears his mother as she uses nurturing, sensitive words to get her point across.

As children, and throughout their socialization period as young adults, boys not only play differently than girls, they talk about different things. Girls talk about people and their relationships with others while boys talk about activities and who is the best at each endeavor. Since young boys become introduced to sports at an early age, their socialization concerning winning forms quickly. One positive outcome of this competitiveness in young boys is that they tend to hold fewer grudges, both as young men and in adult life. Young boys learn that "when the game's over, it's over; let's benefit from our mistakes and look forward to the next game!" Girls tend to hold on to old hurts for a longer time.

Research has provided us with one humorous fact concerning the development of speech in children. In taped conversations of two-year-olds, studies find that 100 percent of a little girl's conversation is words. Sixty percent of a little boy's conversation is words; the other 40 percent consists of sounds ("uhmmmmmmm" or "urrrrrrk"). Wonder if these move up into adult conversations?

With such vast differences during their early socialization periods, it stands to reason that when children become adults they experience a difficult time communicating with members of the opposite sex.

How well does one know and understand the opposite gender? Differences in body language, appearance, proxemics, thinking styles, and negotiating styles make each gender unique and interesting. Answer "true" or "false" to each question to determine your level of understanding gender differences.

GENDER DIFFERENCES IN COMMUNICATION

_____ 1. Men interrupt more and will answer a question even when not addressed to them.

_____ 2. Through their body language, women make themselves less confrontational than men.

_____ 3. Men ask for assistance less often than women do.

_____ 4. A woman gestures away from her body.

_____ 5. Men engage in more eye contact during conversations.

_____ 6. Men prefer side-by-side interactions.

_____ 7. Men speak approximately 9,000 words per day, while women speak approximately 25,000 words per day.

_____ 8. Women are more likely to invade another's personal space.

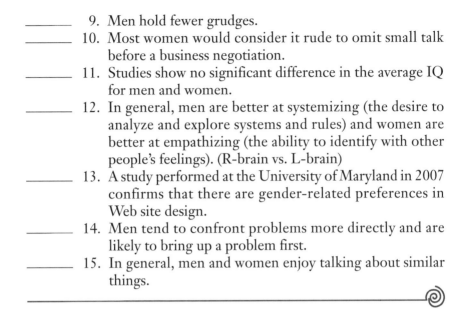

_____ 9. Men hold fewer grudges.

_____ 10. Most women would consider it rude to omit small talk before a business negotiation.

_____ 11. Studies show no significant difference in the average IQ for men and women.

_____ 12. In general, men are better at systemizing (the desire to analyze and explore systems and rules) and women are better at empathizing (the ability to identify with other people's feelings). (R-brain vs. L-brain)

_____ 13. A study performed at the University of Maryland in 2007 confirms that there are gender-related preferences in Web site design.

_____ 14. Men tend to confront problems more directly and are likely to bring up a problem first.

_____ 15. In general, men and women enjoy talking about similar things.

As is evident from the previous exercise, men and women communicate differently. Each gender tends to focus on separate strategies and different parts of nonverbal communication to get the message heard. As stated earlier, women use nonverbal communication to make connections. Men engage in nonverbal communication behaviors that parallel actions associated with dominance, power, and winning.

negotiating styles: women circumnavigate; men go direct

During negotiations, women tend to be less direct than men. Because of the importance that they place on relationships, women want to connect on some other basis before getting down to the business of negotiating. A woman considers it rude to get down to business immediately without first engaging in social conversation. In other words, they circumnavigate and take longer to get where they want to go.

Men, on the other hand, prefer to get right to the point, with only a minimum of trivial conversation. Their small talk is seemingly to build credibility for themselves. For this reason, men are comfortable starting off negotiations by talking about their position and their accomplishments.

Women are typically more interested in working out solutions that satisfy everyone; therefore, negotiations are usually a longer process for them. Men, on the other hand, tend to be impatient during negotiations. Once they find an acceptable solution to the majority of their discussion points, they are ready to move on. Experienced negotiators recognize that women find it more difficult to negotiate with people they dislike. Men only experience slight discomforts or next to no difficulty during negotiations or when conversing with those that they dislike.

Once a person is aware of his own style of negotiating and the other gender's style, he can then prepare accordingly. Although it is important to be true to oneself, once a person realizes that another person's style of negotiating is quite different from his own, it might be beneficial to adjust his style as necessary. Even though some women feel uncomfortable discussing their credentials, it is wise early in the negotiation to establish some of the facts of why they belong at the bargaining table.

gender differences in processing information and talk time

As women make decisions, they tend to process and think of options out loud. Men process internally until they come up with a solution. Because men typically do not participate in this verbal brainstorming, women think that men are being unresponsive to their suggestions. Men often think that women are looking for approval when they process out loud and frequently see this as a sign of weakness.

Men take up more time and space at meetings. During negotiations, men talk more than women and interrupt more often. Research, though, indicates that during the typical day, men speak approximately 11,000 words and women speak approximately 25,000 words. The excessive female wordage is composed of the "tag endings" that women attach to sentences.

People have typically equated bulk and mass to power. Men walk into a conference room and immediately establish some degree of authority because of their height or weight. A woman has the disadvantage here. She is typically smaller in size than the men. She sits with her legs and arms crossed across her body and appears nonconfrontational. A woman at a conference table can give the impression that she is taking up more space by distributing her material further out than usual, squaring her shoulders back, holding her head high, and sometimes extending one of her arms slightly on the back of her chair.

gender differences in nonverbal communication styles

A woman will nod her head to show that she is listening. Men sometimes leave the conversation thinking that the head nod meant agreement and are surprised to find out later that the woman did not agree at all. When a woman is speaking with a man who stays in the neutral position and does not say anything, she interprets his behavior as being bored or not understanding what she is saying. This leads to the woman becoming uncomfortable and repeating everything she says or asking the man each time if he understood what she just said. The man then interprets this as insecurity, leading him to think that the woman is not assertive or confident as a leader.

Women will use more direct eye contact in conversations to create a connection; men sometimes see this intense direct eye contact as a challenge to their power or position. Proper eye contact does not mean just gazing into the eyes; it means sincerely looking with the intent of letting the other person know that you are listening. Sixty-five to 70 percent of all eye contact during business interactions should be in the "eye-forehead-nose" triangle. Shifty eyes and excessive blinking are indicative of someone who is insecure with what he is saying.

Typically, men prefer approaches from the side and women prefer approaches from the front at the start of a negotiation. Since a woman tends to be distrustful of someone who sneaks up on her from the side, she prefers a face-to-face interaction. A woman needs to feel that the other negotiator is being upfront with her. Seating selection is also important in the negotiating process. If a person has already met his client and knows that he is right handed, he should attempt to sit to his right. If the client is left handed, sit to his left.

Once seated, whether male or female, a person should keep his hands from his face and hair. There is nothing positive that fingers can do above the neck while a person is negotiating with a client. While seated, it is best to keep both feet on the floor. It helps to maintain control and good body posture. Negotiators perceive people who constantly cross and uncross their legs and feet as more nervous and less credible.

In meetings, men gain the floor more often and keep the floor for longer periods of time. When women do ask a question, they take less time asking it than do men. Women are also less likely to ask multiple questions and are more likely than men to phrase their question in personal terms. In general, people are more likely to perceive those who talk more as dominant and controlling, but those who intelligently ask open-ended questions in decision-making groups are the ones who typically become the leaders. Participants in negotiations perceive interrupters as successful and driving but less socially acceptable and less pleasing than the interrupted speaker.

Building rapport is difficult when people speak at different rates, but if a person can get on pace with the other person's speaking style in a first contact meeting, his negotiating partner will see him in a more positive light. People who speak slowly consider those who speak quickly to be aggressive and often offensive. Positive attributes credited to the fast-paced communicator include intelligence and quick thinking. People who speak quickly normally perceive slower communicators as being uninspiring and dreary, but gentle and caring. The fast-paced communicator often becomes impatient with the pace of the slower communicator. It is generally easier for people who normally speak quickly to slow down than it is for people who speak slowly to speak more quickly.

Women known to have prior experience in a field or expertise related to a task show increased verbal and nonverbal behaviors in mixed-sex groups. In several carefully controlled studies, males evaluated the assertive behavior exhibited by females as positively as the same behavior exhibited by males. Research further suggests that "the healthiest and best-liked individuals, male or female, are assertive, decisive, and intellectual, rather than nurturant, responsive and emotional."

Understanding gender difference in communication styles is important for two reasons: first, to determine the meaning of what the opposite sex negotiator is saying, and, second, to help a person get his own message across. Being unable to decode nonverbal communication is similar to listening to the news on the radio and only hearing 3 out of every 10 words spoken. The listener will misunderstand what he hears and generally feel frustrated by the experience.

•••• Body Movements ••••
(Gestures, Facial Expression, Posture)

Men	*Women*
1. take up more space	1. take up less space
2. gesture away from their body	2. gesture toward their body
3. assume more reclined positions when sitting and lean backward when listening	3. assume more forward positions when seated and lean forward when listening
4. display frowning and squinting when listening	4. display smiling and head-nodding when listening
5. use touch to direct or assert power	5. associate touch with warmth and affection
6. interrupt others and allow fewer interruptions	6. interrupt less and allow more interruptions
7. have more monotonous speech (use approximately 3 tones when speaking)	7. sound more emotional (use approximately 5 tones when speaking)
8. talk at a slower rate of speech	8. talk at a faster rate of speech
9. make direct accusations (You didn't call!)	9. make indirect accusations (Why didn't you ever call?)

Men (*continued*)	**Women** (*continued*)
10. say "right" or "okay" as interjections	10. say "um hum" as interjections
11. give more direct commands (Get me the paper!)	11. use softer command terms (Would you mind getting me the paper?)
12. make declarative statements (It's a nice day.)	12. use "tag endings" on statements (It's a nice day, isn't it?)
13. use fewer emotional verbs	13. use emotional verbs: "feel, hope"
14. tend to lecture more . . . monologue	14. use give and take in conversations . . . dialogue
15. have an analytical approach to problems (left brain)	15. have an emotional approach to problems (right brain)
16. hold fewer grudges	16. hold more grudges
17. rarely bring up incidents from the past in a disagreement	17. bring up incidents from the past in disagreements
18. are less likely to ask for help; try to figure things out on their own	18. are likely to ask for help in solving problems
19. prefer side-by-side interactions	19. prefer face-to-face conversations
20. take verbal rejection less personally	20. take verbal rejection more personally
21. want to get down to the business at hand as quickly as possible	21. want to get to know the other person first, before negotiation begins
22. are comfortable talking about their accomplishments	22. are not comfortable listing their accomplishments
23. believe the outcome of this negotiation takes priority over future dealings	23. consider the long-term relationship as important as the outcome of of any single negotiation

⑤trategies to bridge gender differences and value diverse styles

Not everyone fits these generalizations. The above are cultural norms based on research that shows that a large majority of men and women display these characteristics. But if a person grasps the importance of effective gender communication styles and gender equality in the workplace, he can start making a difference today using the following gender communication strategies:

Men, be aware of how much time and space you demand in meetings or group interactions. Make room for the contributions of women. When asked for a decision or your opinion by a woman, let her know nonverbally that you are in the process of thinking about it so that she knows that she is heard.

Women, get comfortable with asserting more space for yourself. Do not second guess your opinions by using tag endings on sentences. Never undercut your message with negative nonverbal actions; adopt a relaxed, but firm posture.

Learn about male and female styles of communication and be able to use both. With the complexity and diversity of situations in today's world, an individual needs knowledge of both styles to aid himself personally and professionally. The better an individual "can read" the opposite gender, the more effective he is as a negotiator.

Answers to *Gender Differences in Communication* exercise:
1. T; **2.** T; **3.** T; **4.** F; **5.** F; **6.** F; **7.** F; **8.** F; **9.** T; **10.** T; **11.** T; **12.** T; **13.** T; **14.** F; **15.** F

Cultural Communication Differences During Sales and Negotiations: Handshakes, Headshakes, Bowing, Hugging, or Kissing

11

Americans who have the greatest success in negotiating business abroad and with other nationalities are those who have learned how to strike a balance between capitalizing upon the strengths and advantages they enjoy as Americans and showing a credible appreciation and understanding of the social and business customs of other cultures.

As the global village continues to shrink and cultures collide, it is essential to become more sensitive, more aware, and more observant of the myriad motions, gestures, and body language that surround us each day. Without gestures, our world would be stationary and colorless. Visually, the world is a giddy montage of vivid gestures: traffic police, street vendors, expressway drivers, children on the playground, and athletes with their exuberant hugging, clenched fists, and "high fives." People all over the world use their hands, head, and bodies to communicate expressively.

At no time in history has there been so great a need for international negotiating skills. To be effective as an organization and as an individual within these organizations, it is imperative that people learn to think globally. The multitude of international business arrangements accomplished daily requires individuals to become effective world-class negotiators.

To be convinced of a person's involvement in the global economy, all a person need do is think about his average day. He wakes up wrapped in his Italian sheets, brushes his teeth with Close-Up toothpaste, eats a Kiss muffin, sprays on his Clive Christian perfume, checks his Rolex watch, and rushes out of the door to his Mercedes that is filled with Shell gasoline. A non-U.S. company has made each of these consumer products.

It is not unusual to work for an organization that does business in many different countries. The best example of a multinational enterprise, with facilities in virtually every foreign country, is the U.S. Postal

Service. At present most people have specific concerns about successfully negotiating with a counterpart in one particular country. Over time, people will become concerned and eager to negotiate with individuals from several countries in the world.

What makes global negotiations different?

Anthropologists point out that cultures are different because various peoples had to deal with diverse circumstances to meet their human needs: different climates, different resources, and different terrain. Over the years, the complex array of solutions to problems created the patterns in cultural behaviors. One can only begin to understand the customs of a nation by analyzing and considering the difference between the past, present, and future of that nation.

Numerous "macro-factors," such as politics and the economic climate of the region, influence international business negotiations. Attention to these factors helps one access the overall business and organizational climate in which the negotiation is taking place. The cultural factors of a particular region are more important than any other key influence in determining cultural behavior. One must explore the differences in pace, style, strategies, and nonverbal communication before the international negotiation process.

PACE; TIME

Americans come across as always being in a hurry, rarely stopping to enjoy the present. People of other nationalities observe that Americans treat time as a valuable, tangible, and limited resource. For a typical appointment in America, a negotiator would be on time. To arrive too early could suggest anxiousness or eagerness to the client. In America, a long wait communicates disrespect or an extreme inequality in status. People expect that business meetings in the United States will take place within one or two hours. If phone calls or other distractions interrupt the meeting, clients will resent the loss of time. Panic may even set in if the parties do not meet the objective of the meeting near the end of the appointment. If the meeting proceeds as scheduled with a conclusion, all involved participants will feel a sense of accomplishment.

Negotiations are likely to progress in this same manner in Australia, Germany, Switzerland, Israel, and Scandinavia. In many other parts of the world time is not the issue. Meetings may begin with long socializing over many cups of coffee or tea. This lengthy socializing may take hours, and perhaps even several meetings will occur during which no mention of the business objective takes place. Americans need to know that during these apparently aimless conversations important progress is occurring toward establishing credibility and rapport.

While an American visitor to Saudi Arabia is likely to find that his appointment is not a private affair, he should also know that an Arab may take a deadline as an insult. Since Japanese invest much research and analysis into a decision, a delay means something quite different. Japanese negotiators consider a group of issues rather than resolving issues one at a time. They will never give a direct "no" to a proposal and consider direct negative statements quite rude. Instead, the Japanese negotiator might offer a suggestion such as "That will require further thought" and ask for another meeting.

Tactfully asking if the meeting will take place on "Mexican time" or "American time" in Mexico can help to clarify the beginning time. Saudi clients might have a negotiator flown into a major city or exotic resort for a meeting, only to delay for days. The positive aspect of the delayed meeting date is that they graciously grant compensation for time and expenses.

STYLE; STRATEGY

Negotiating strategies employed and formality of approach differ from region to region. Germany, the United Kingdom, Switzerland, and Japan all expect a high degree of formality with specific, well-organized, data-oriented presentations. Emphasis on broad concepts is much more effective in Latin America or in the Middle East. Even presentation audiences react in different ways across cultures. Some are very engaging and are willing to participate in exercises and question and answer sessions; others are the opposite. A Japanese audience participant might close his eyes while listening, a U.S. audience usually applauds when the speaker makes a good point, and a Saudi might do nothing at all. Since silence in Japan is golden and often used as a negotiating strategy, a client should avoid the temptation to jump in and fill the silence.

Three distinct concession patterns emerge among countries. Negotiators from the United States, South Africa, and Brazil select a "hard-nosed" pattern where negotiators reluctantly concede. Negotiators from Australia, New Zealand, Taiwan, and Thailand like the second pattern, which is one of "de-escalation." These negotiators are generous at first and then taper off. The third pattern is one of "escalation." Negotiators from Indonesia, the Philippines, India, and Kenya prefer this pattern. These negotiations begin with a low amount, with the offer increasing at each negotiating session.

NONVERBAL COMMUNICATION

Understanding the unspoken language of a specific culture is important for two reasons. First, it helps determine the meaning of what the international negotiator is saying, and second it helps the North American negotiator get his own message across. Body language varies widely among cultures, from handshakes to headshakes, bowing to smiling, hugging to kissing, and eye contact and posture to personal space. American, German, Canadian, and Russian negotiators have very firm handshakes. There are usually several pumps of the arm, and the strong grip delivers an unspoken message of confidence. The French, however, consider one pump sufficient, and the pressure is generally lighter. A Japanese business person shakes hands with the arm fully extended; a bow usually accompanies the handshake. In the Middle East, negotiators shake hands with their free hand placed on the forearm of the other person. Even though the Chinese have a softer handshake, they are quietly effective in the firmness of their positions. Businesswomen meeting with colleagues in Israel should not offer a handshake if the counterparts are Orthodox Jews, as the religion forbids physical contact of any kind with a woman not of their immediate family. In India, male colleagues automatically shake hands, but businesswomen make the decision whether or not to extend their hands along with a vocal greeting.

Although shaking one's head from side to side usually indicates "no," even this simple gesture does not have a universal meaning. Bulgarians shake their head in the method of the American "no" to indicate agreement. People from southern India and Pakistan move their heads from side to side to express a variety of meanings, such as "you're welcome," "goodbye," enjoyment, or that the person acknowledges what another person has said.

In Japan, people bow with their hands at their sides. The depth of the bow relates to the level of respect due to the other person. People from Cambodia and Laos bow with their hands placed in front of their chests. People from Pakistan use the *salaam;* they bow with the palm of their right hand on their forehead.

While people from other cultures may interpret a smile as insincere, North Americans smile automatically when greeting others. Asian people smile less than Westerners, and in Korea, people consider it inappropriate for adults to smile in public. For Koreans, a smile usually indicates embarrassment, not pleasure.

Native Hawaiians hug and exchange breaths in a custom called "aha." Latinos will usually hug upon greeting (the *abrazo*). In Cuba, Portugal, Spain, Italy, Eastern Europe, and in the Middle East, men exchange kisses on the cheek. For the Maori of New Zealand, a traditional greeting includes pressing together the noses (the *hongi*), and a cry of welcome (the *karanga*).

People in Western cultures make intermittent eye contact while speaking to demonstrate interest and trustworthiness. Those in the Middle East use very intense and prolonged eye contact to gauge another person's intentions. They typically move in very close to see the other person's eyes better. In Japan, people interpret direct eye contact as an invasion of a person's privacy and an act of rudeness.

The amount of personal space that North Americans require is about the length of an arm. The French, Latin Americans, and Arabs need less personal space, while Germans and Japanese need more. For Japanese, bowing too close to each other could be dangerous! Around the world, social status, gender, or age may also influence the size of one's personal space. Awareness of the level of personal space required is crucial; if not gauged properly, inappropriate proximity or distance can lead to misunderstandings and interpretation as an insult.

In the Middle East, it is extremely offensive to point the bottom of one's foot in another person's direction; therefore, sitting cross-legged might be a bad idea. In any culture, it is not wise for the negotiator to leave his hands in his pockets or to lean against a wall or door when speaking to someone.

To obtain the true meaning of a nonverbal gesture, look for *clusters of behavior*. If a counterpart asks, "Is this your best price?" and folds his arms, he does not necessarily mean he's being defensive. The room may feel cold or he is simply comfortable sitting that way. If, however, he suddenly folds his arms, moves in his seat, clears his throat, and starts blinking rapidly, then the negotiator needs to probe the situation further.

ⓖuidelines for cross culture negotiations

A negotiator needs to interpret the other person's clues as that person intends them. A Japanese woman is showing polite respect, not coldness, when she avoids eye contact and maintains her distance. Conversely, a man from an Arabic background is being sincere, not threatening, when he looks at the negotiator intently and speaks with exaggerated gestures.

Do not make assumptions! A person needs to ask when he does not understand a cultural norm. Questioning helps to avoid misunderstandings and embarrassment. Test your cultural intelligence (CQ) with the exam that follows:

GLOBAL BUSINESS: CUSTOMS AND ETIQUETTE

Cultural Intelligence

1. To impress your Hispanic mother-in-law while visiting her home in Mexico, you take her some beautiful yellow marigolds. (T/F)

2. Hand holding between men is acceptable in Saudi Arabia. (T/F)

3. The bullfight is the most popular sport in Argentina. (T/F)

4. People consider the number four good luck in China and Japan. (T/F)

5. Brazilians speak Spanish. (T/F)

6. To beckon another person in Spain, you would turn your palm down and wave your fingers or whole hand. (T/F)

7. You are negotiating with an Asian colleague, and he says, "That will be difficult" or "That requires further study." What does he mean?

8. In Europe, business people expect an exchange of business cards as an introduction. (T/F)

9. Dinner reservations in Spain are generally for 8:00 P.M. (T/F)

10. Hindus do not eat beef, and Muslims do not eat pork. (T/F)

11. One should use both hands to accept business cards in:
    a. India
    b. Africa
    c. Japan

12. Making a circle with the thumb and index finger:
    a. Means money in Japan
    b. Is vulgar in Brazil
    c. Is impolite in Russia
    d. All of the above

13. In general, Canadians write the day first, then the month, then the year (e.g., December 3, 2007, is written 3.12.07). (T/F)

14. Which of the following people use the expression "sitting near the window" to refer to employees the company is retiring?
    a. Arabs
    b. Japanese
    c. Spaniards

15. The Chinese are enthusiastic applauders; they may even applaud others during the greeting. If a person receives applause in this fashion, it is the custom to return it. (T/F)

16. The Northern European countries are not sticklers for punctuality. (T/F)

17. In the U.S. business negotiations occur at lightning speed in comparison to many cultures. U.S. sales people may even bring final contracts to their first meeting with prospective clients. (T/F)

18. In Denmark, what is the word used for toasting when drinking?

    _____

19. To perform the traditional Indian greeting, the *namaste*, a person holds the palms of his hands together below his chin and nods or bows slightly. (T/F)

20. Personal space is rather limited in China. During conversations the Chinese will stand much closer than Westerners. (T/F)

21. To signal "one" in Germany, hold the thumb upright. (T/F)

22. Latinos are status-conscious during negotiations. One member of your negotiating team should be from higher-level management. During introductions, one should mention his university degrees; he should stay in superior hotels and eat at good restaurants. (T/F)

23. Guests need to be careful about expressing admiration for small but expensive possessions in the home of a Middle Eastern person (Saudi Arabia, Israel, Egypt, Syria, Iran, Iraq, Jordan, Lebanon, etc.). (T/F)

24. Muslims, whose Islamic culture rests upon the teaching of Mohammed, pray _____ times a day, bowing to the ground toward Mecca.

25. _____ is the second largest country in the world, after Russia.

26. In Colombia and Mexico, individuals bear two family names: The last name is the mother's family name, and the middle name is the father's family name and the official surname. Therefore, Pedro Munoz Gomez is called Senor Munoz. (T/F)

27. _____ (country) (because of its vast length—over 4,000 miles long) is sometimes called the "Switzerland of South America" for its natural beauty and many different climate changes, from subtropical in the north, to subarctic in the south.

28. Common greetings in _____ are *Guten morgen* (Good morning), *Guten tag* (Good afternoon) and *Guten abend* (Good evening).

29. Concerning chopstick etiquette, it is customary to stand them up in your bowl of rice. (T/F)

30. In Japan, a smile can mean pleasure, but it can also indicate self-control, as when used to hide displeasure. (T/F)

31. In Kenya and Africa, what is the greeting for hello?

    _____

32. In what country(s) do you remove your shoes before entering a mosque?

    _____

33. In China, what gesture is appropriate when meeting someone?

    _____

34. In the Middle East, which is the only hand that one can use when eating?

    _____

35. Avoid using the word "English" when talking about the people in England, Scotland, and Wales. One should use: _____.

36. Why isn't it fine to cross your ankle over your knee in Muslim countries and in Buddhist cultures?

    _____

    _____

    _____

37. What is the preferred reference for people from China, Japan, and Vietnam?

_____

38. Canada spans five time zones. (T/F)

39. In Greece, what are the rules for greeting people?

_____

_____

_____

40. Germans take great pride in their automobiles. (T/F)

41. People consider it bad manners to talk with their hands in Finland. (T/F)

42. A sideways movement of the head, which resembles the negative shake of Americans, indicates the "yes" of a Greek, Turk, or Bulgarian. (T/F)

43. British people gesture very little when speaking; they do not move their hands about, and they hold their heads high. (T/F)

44. Should one give gifts wrapped in red in China or Japan?

_____

45. In India, the people consider the head the seat of the soul. Never touch someone else's head, not even to pat the hair of a child. (T/F)

46. When dining, Italians keep both hands above the table. (T/F)

47. About 65 percent of _____ people have last names that end in "sen" (for instance, Andersen, Christensen, Hansen).

48. Expect Kuwaitis to sit and stand very close. They may rest a hand on your shoulder or even tap your forearm with a finger. (T/F)

49. People use the basic greeting *xin chao* (pronounced "seen-chow") primarily in _____.

50. The most powerful, best understood, most disarming, and most international body language signal of all is the smile. (T/F)

Body language one-liners, especially common among North Americans, follow:

Action		*Meaning*
Toes pointed outward	➡	Confidence
Toes pointed inward	➡	Submission
A jutting chin	➡	Belligerence
Lip and nail biting	➡	Disappointment
Lip licking	➡	Nervousness
Foot tapping	➡	Impatience
Leaning backward	➡	A relaxed attitude
Leaning forward	➡	Interest
Open palms	➡	Honesty
Rubbing hands together	➡	Excitement
Rubbing left eye	➡	Deceit
Scratching neck	➡	Uncertainty
Arms folded	➡	Defiance and refusal

Answers to *Global Business Customs and Etiquette* exercise:

1. F; **2.** T; **3.** F; **4.** F; **5.** F; **6.** T; **7.** "no"; **8.** T; **9.** F (later; 10:00 P.M.); **10.** T; **11.** C; **12.** D; **13.** T; **14.** B; **15.** T; **16.** F; **17.** T; **18.** Skol; **19.** T; **20.** T; **21.** T; **22.** T; **23.** T; **24.** 5; **25.** Canada; **26.** T; **27.** Chile; **28.** Germany; **29.** T; **30.** T; **31.** Jambo; **32.** Middle Eastern countries; **33.** Bow; **34.** Right; **35.** British; **36.** Soles of the feet are the lowest, therefore the dirtiest part of the body; **37.** Asians; **38.** T; **39.** None; they hug, kiss, shake hands; **40.** T; **41.** T; **42.** T; **43.** T; **44.** China; **45.** T; **46.** T; **47.** Denmark; **48.** T; **49.** Vietnam; **50.** T

Power Seating: Strategic Office Layout–Desks, Chairs, and Seating Arrangements

Seating arrangements can have a profound effect on the environment of a meeting and on the ultimate outcome of a negotiation. A person can create the illusion of power or equality in his relationship-building efforts by where he sits and where he seats others at meetings. The strategic placing of people involved in a discussion, regardless of the objective or format, requires careful planning. In other words, there is a "seating" language under the nonverbal communication umbrella.

Seating arrangements should support the goal of the meeting. Jean M. Rowan, president of The Bottom Line, a coaching and training institute for professionals in personal marketing and presentation skills, suggests answering specific questions when considering the characteristics of the table and seating arrangements prior to a meeting.

- Is the meeting formal or informal?
- Will there be a designated leader?
- How many people will be attending?
- What is the desired degree of individual involvement and interaction?
- Are there potential controversial issues on the agenda?
- Are there probable conflicts among the participants?

The drawing at the top of the next page shows a table and six chairs. As a prospect enters a room, he sees the negotiator seated at the position marked "X." Decide which chair each of the following individuals should occupy by placing the appropriate letter on the seat.

a. A person enters the room to continue work on a spreadsheet that he began with the negotiator last week. Place an "A" on the appropriate seat.

b. An employee enters the room to negotiate renewal of his yearly contract. Place a "B" on the appropriate seat.

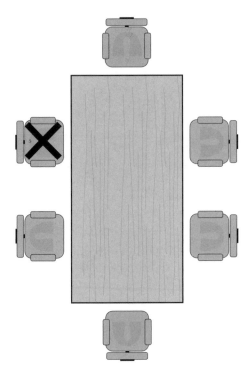

c. The company accountant arrives for a friendly refresher course concerning employee expense reports. Place a "C" on the appropriate seat.

d. An administrative assistant comes into the corporate conference meeting to record minutes of the gathering. Place a "D" on the appropriate seat.

It is readily evident that there are obvious positions beneficial for each situation. A person can direct or control responses in meetings through proper seating arrangements and room ambience. The ambience of the venue sets the stage, determines the credibility of the meeting, and establishes the degree of engagement. It governs the level of communication and often becomes an integral part of the message.

Employee "A" should sit in the most cooperative position, that is, next to the negotiator (next to the seat marked "X") because no barriers are necessary. People who already know each other and are in a partnership relationship to accomplish a task use this "Cooperative" position. Since they are not competing with each other, there is no need to keep an eye on what the other person is doing. Since eye contact is a method to control interaction and conversation, another observation concerning meeting seating highly advises placing opponents on the same side of the table but several seats away from each other. The meeting leader will find that the opposition is greatly diffused since eye contact between the two bickering parties is difficult. Opponents gain strength by playing off one another, so, without eye contact, they are less likely to stir up trouble and more likely to join in a fair discussion.

Place employee "B" in the position directly in front of the negotiator. Since people tend to sit opposite those they are competing against, this "Competitive/Defensive" position is ideal for each party to take a firm stand on his own point of view and attempt to eventually see things eye-to-eye. The table serves as a solid barrier between the two individuals and helps each to establish his territory. During a disciplinary interview, individuals may even choose to sit at opposite ends of a long rectangular table. Accidentally pushing items into someone else's space during a confrontational debate is as much an invasion of space as if someone had reached across the table and punched the other person. Territorial rights are as important in business meetings as they are in informal situations. Two people seated at a restaurant table will mark their boundaries with the salt and pepper shaker and sugar bowl.

The proper place for person "C" is in the seat diagonally to the left of the negotiator, at the end of the table. Individuals who are engaged in a friendly, casual conversation favor this "Corner" position. It allows for unlimited eye contact and is a perfect opportunity to use and observe numerous gestures.

Administrative assistant "D" sits diagonally to the right of the negotiator. People who take this "Independent" position feel autonomous and do not wish to interact with the others at the table. They do not want to be involved in the conversation. It is a typical position taken by people in a cafeteria who have to share a table; even though the two have to share space, they are not anxious to share conversation.

A ➡ **The cooperative position**

B ➡ **The competitive/defensive position**

C ➡ **The corner position**

D ➡ **The independent position**

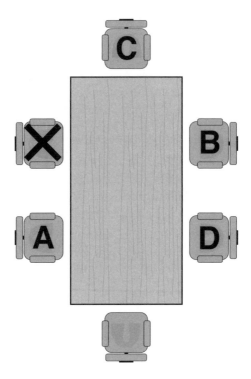

Try the exercise again and attempt to visualize each interaction with the negotiator sitting in a different seat. Determine which position offers the best compromise between the overly formal and the too casual. Consider a situation where a meeting leader is insecure about his position and chooses a seat in the middle of the conference table. Without good eye contact with all the participants, the leader will lose much of his ability to control the discussion. Without control, the group will lose its focus and generally disintegrate into sidebar discussions among subgroups. Concerning seating arrangements, it is important to note that most people are creatures of habit and, given the choice, generally like to sit in the same place at every meeting. In fact, a person can get very irritated if someone sits in "his" seat. Once an individual observes this behavior in one of his colleagues, to deter conflict, he should allow the territorial person to be seated first.

Square Table Seating

Those whose relationship with each other is competitive will sit facing each other. Those whose relationship or task is a cooperative one will tend to sit diagonally from each other. Since behavior is predictable, one can easily use square tables to encourage specific desired behaviors. Even though a person seated on the left of the host is in a cooperative position, the highest amount of cooperation usually comes from the individual seated to the right of the host. The most resistance typically comes from the person seated directly opposite the meeting host.

ROUND TABLE SEATING

Round table seating arrangements foster a feeling of contribution for all meeting participants because they create a sense of belonging and involvement. Equal input of ideas is easier when people sit in a circular pattern that de-emphasizes the importance of a leader. Since each person can claim the same amount of table territory, this type of seating is ideal for encouraging discussion among people who are of equal rank. Removing the table and sitting in a circle also promotes the same result.

An indirect placement of power occurs if someone gets placed as the acting head of the round table. This status position subconsciously alters the power and authority of each other person. Individuals seated on either side of the power position are nonverbally granted the next highest amount of power, the one on his right having a little more power than the one on the left. The amount of power diminishes relative to the distance that each person's seat is from the indirect power position.

The person seated directly across the table from the power position is, in effect, in the competitive/defensive position and is likely to be the one who is the most disagreeable. Many of today's business executives use both square and round tables for their daily activities. They use the square desk, which is usually the work desk, for business discussions, brief conversations, or confrontations. They use the round table, sometimes a coffee table, to create an informal, relaxed atmosphere that encourages involvement.

RECTANGULAR TABLE SEATING

In this moderately formal, business-like atmosphere, the leader should sit in the control position at the end of the table that is at the greatest distance from the door. Since either end of the table is a control position, the closest ally to the leader or the toughest antagonist should sit in the opposite control position. The rectangular table seating arrangement invites formation of teams. Typically one side of the

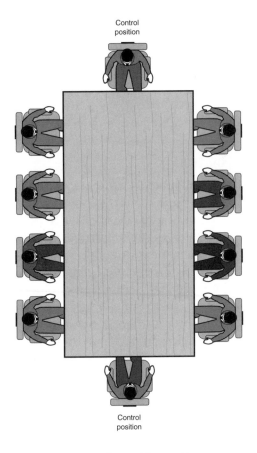

Control
position

Control
position

rectangular table seating

table opposes the other side of the table. This parallel arrangement enhances discussion between participants, especially those seated across from each other.

U-SHAPED TABLE SEATING

The leadership position in this type of seating arrangement is in the center at the base of the U-shape. With a clear vision of all the meeting participants, the power position individual is able to dominate proceedings. Individuals placed on either side of the leader also have significant psychological control of the group. Secondary power positions are at each tip of the U-shape. This formal atmosphere is excellent for facilitating group discussions. Meeting attendees should not

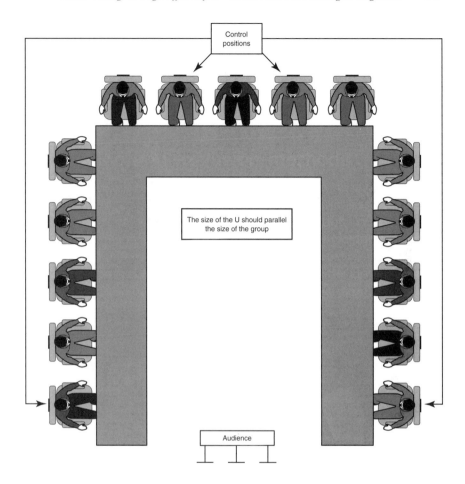

U-shaped table seating

sit inside the U; it decreases participant interaction. Most importantly, the size of the U table must match the size of the group.

OVAL TABLE SEATING

This arrangement combines the attributes of circular and rectangular seating assemblies. The two leadership positions are at either end of the oval. There is also an option for the leader of the group to sit in the middle along the length of the table. This type of arrangement is less formal, promotes discussion, and allows for abundant eye contact.

oval table seating

❶eam seating plans

For anything other than extremely formal negotiations, a team of five is the accepted maximum. The "across the table" approach, in which the teams sit facing each other, is customary, and negotiators favor it when they want to emphasize their separate identities. The labels of the key members of a seasoned negotiating team are: leader, good guy, bad guy, hard liner, and sweeper. The leader sits centrally, uniting all team members. The good guy sits on the right side of the leader to form a friendly, approachable unit. The hard liner sits on the left side of the leader since his skills complement those of the leader. The sweeper sits on the left of the hard liner, typically at the far end of the negotiation table. It is his task to analyze the reactions of the other team members. The bad guy, or most challenging to win over, sits at the other end of the table seemingly separated from the rest of the team.

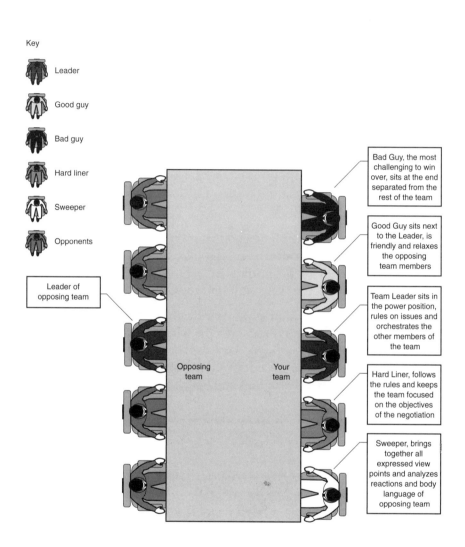

team seating plan

•••• *Roles of Team Members* ••••

Role	Responsibility
LEADER	The person with the most expertise who conducts the negotiation and occasionally calls on others. He orchestrates the other members of the team and rules on matters.
GOOD GUY	The person with whom most members of the opposite team will identify. He relaxes the opposing team members by expressing sympathy and understanding.
HARD LINER	This team member takes a hard line on everything. He uses stalling tactics to delay progress and keeps the remainder of the team focused on the objectives of the negotiations.
BAD GUY	Opposite of the good guy. This person's role is to make the opposition feel that agreement is impossible. He tries to intimidate the opposition and expose their weaknesses by undermining their argument.
SWEEPER	This person summarizes and brings together all the expressed points of view. He prevents the discussion from straying too far from the main issues and suggests tactics to get out of a deadlocked negotiation. He also analyzes reactions and body language of opposing team members.

Reading basic body language signals of conference table participants

One member of the negotiating team should have the assignment of detecting body language signals given off by the opposing team. Eye contact is one of the most important aspects of body language, but understanding what the opponents are thinking is a tremendous asset. By reading the signals given off by their gestures and overall posture, a person can gain insightful information concerning the opposing team's interest, resistance, or decisions.

basic body language gestures

business dinners

It may look like lunch or dinner, but it is still business. At a restaurant or dinner party, the negotiator achieves a better chance of receiving a positive decision if the client feels relaxed and free of tension and has lowered all of his defensive barriers. To achieve this end, follow a few simple rules.

Whether dining at home or at a restaurant, the client should sit with his back to a solid wall or screen. Research shows that respiration, heart rate, brain wave frequencies, and blood pressure rapidly increase when a person sits with his back to an open door, particularly where others are moving about. Tension further increases if the person's back is toward an open window at ground level. Round dinner tables are best for restaurant negotiations. To secure a captive audience, the client should have an obscured view of other people as much as possible.

Efficient, smooth flowing restaurants with soft lighting are best for relaxing talk. This informal atmosphere encourages communication and involvement. Restaurants that have bright lighting, crowded tables, and servers who habitually bang plates, knives, and forks are a distraction for successful negotiations.

During dinner meetings, it is best to leave the table only between courses. A negotiator needs to remember to place his napkin in his chair if he has to leave during the dinner and to the right of his plate once the meal is finished. He should also wait for everyone to be served before beginning his meal. When it comes to picking up the tab, the person who did the inviting is responsible for the check. If it is a joint meeting, the participants should divide the check. A negotiator having dinner with someone who is offering him valuable advice or services should pick up the tab.

GLOBAL BUSINESS: CUSTOMS AND ETIQUETTE

1. Whose name do you say first when introducing your sister to your boss?
2. At a business luncheon you meet the CEO of a prestigious corporation. After a brief conversation you give him your business card. Is this correct?
3. Would you find your salad plate to the right or left of your dinner plate?
4. When entering a cab with an important client, you position yourself so the client is seated curbside. Is this correct?
5. Your host serves champagne with dessert at a dinner party. You simply cannot drink champagne, yet you know the host will be offering a toast. Do you:
    a. Tell the waiter, "no champagne"
    b. Turn over your glass
    c. Ask the waiter to pour water into your champagne glass instead
    d. Say nothing and allow the champagne to be poured
6. You are invited to a reception and the invitation states "7:00 P.M. to 9:00 P.M." You should arrive:
    a. At 7:00 P.M.
    b. Anytime between 7:00 P.M. and 9:00 P.M.
    c. Between 7:00 P.M. and 7:30 P.M.
    d. Early and leave early.
7. Pushing back your plate signals that you have finished eating.
8. A man should wait for a business woman to extend her hand for a handshake.
9. During a conversation with four people, do you make eye contact with:
    a. Just the person to whom you are speaking at the moment.
    b. Each of the four, moving your eye contact from one to another.
    c. No one particular person (not looking directly into anyone's eyes).
10. When you greet a visitor in your office, do you:
    a. Say nothing and let her sit where she wishes.
    b. Tell her where to sit.
    c. Say, "Just sit anywhere."

(Answers are at the end of the chapter.)

❶he dynamics of chairs: height, type, size, positioning

Dimensionally speaking, being higher up puts a person in a dominating position. Chair height and seat positioning convey status. People who sit at either end in the jury chairs most often get elected foreman. Employees clearly associate with higher rank the executive known by the term "right-hand man" who aligns himself on the right-hand side of the senior leader. Status further increases for the individual who leans toward the senior executive when he speaks with him. This sideways lean is an index of relaxation and friendliness.

The behavior of people entering offices indicates how they signal their status to others. Low status individuals tend to stay near the door when entering. Higher status people approach the desk. Those of equal status to the executive will come in and sit down next to his desk. If friends drop by for a visit, the executive typically comes out from behind his desk and greets them.

The height of the back of a chair can raise or lower a person's status. The higher the back of the chair, people presume, the greater the power and status of the person sitting in it. Popes, queens, and kings sit in official chairs with backs as high as 8 feet to show their status relative to their subjects. The senior executive usually sits in a high-backed leather chair while his visitor's chair has a low back.

Swivel chairs have more power and status than fixed chairs. They allow the user freedom of movement when he is under pressure and can help hide some of his nervous gestures. Chairs with arm rests, chairs that can lean back, chairs that can rock, and chairs that have wheels are better than chairs that have none.

Status increases when a negotiator adjusts his chair higher off the floor than his competitor's chair. Deep sofas or chairs that are so low that the client's eyes are level with the executive's desk are power ploys to defeat competition. To further reduce the client's status, some negotiators place the visitor's low chair as far away as possible from their own desk. This arrangement gives the aura of not allowing the client in the negotiator's private territory zone.

❶erritorial/ownership gestures

Territorial claims differ from personal space in that a personal zone accompanies the individual while territory is relatively stationary. Territorial space is often the criteria used to establish a territory within any environment. It becomes a man's safety zone where he rests from the severity of defending personal space from invasion. People indicate their ownership of established territory or objects by simply leaning on the object or touching it. Territorial claims occur extremely rapidly. Most audiences, when returning from an intermission, will return to their initial seats. A slight irritation is visibly evident if someone else is occupying a person's particular seat when he returns from the break.

Changing the distance between two people can convey a desire for intimacy, declare a lack of interest, or increase domination. Police interrogators learn that this violation of personal space can nonverbally convey a message. They increase domination by sitting close and crowding a suspect. The invasion of the suspect's personal space tends to give the officer a psychological advantage.

A person's public personal zone, such as an office or a desk, becomes defended territory if he feels invaded. A person who leans in a doorway, or the business executive who puts his feet up on his desk, attempts to show claim to an office or to office furnishings. People also use these annoying gestures as a method of dominance or intimidation when the objects they are leaning on belong to someone else. It is a technique used to intimidate or pressure another person.

Office cubicles do not lend themselves much to allowing the occupant to rearrange his furniture to allow for personal preferences. Nor are they always large enough to allow for a visitor's chair. An extra chair to a pool employee can easily become a symbol of status since it might indicate that he is expecting professional visitors.

Concerning territorial logistics, it is a good idea for a salesperson calling on a customer at his home to ask him, "Which seat is yours?" before he sits down. Sitting in the wrong chair in any setting, can intimidate the client and make him feel ill at ease. Further, proxemics in the home reveal that some rooms are acceptable for public gatherings, others for close friends and relatives, and some are off limits to certain people. Families even leave some rooms in homes untouched, preserved, and ready for only occasional occupancy. Wisely observing family members take their seats before a home setting negotiation can immensely help to assure a more prosperous communication process.

A leg-over-chair gesture seems to reflect an easy-going, relaxed, and carefree attitude, but it actually signifies a person's indifferent or hostile viewpoint and his ownership of a particular chair or space. This annoying negative gesture reflects a person who only cares about himself and his view on a particular subject. An easy way to break someone from this gesture is to hand him something that he cannot reach or ask him to lean across the desk to further study a document.

ⓣerritory at the office

The office owner can arrange office furniture in such a way that he has as much power, status, or control over others as he wishes. Simply sitting behind a desk conveys a sense of power. Positioning the desk so that all who enter must look across it suggests control. To create an accessible, open door image, a desk should be placed in such a way that the occupant's back is to the door so that he must turn around to greet his visitors. This arrangement ends boundaries between the occupant and his visitor. Textures of office furniture are also indicators of status. A wooden desk gives off an entirely different impression than a metal desk does.

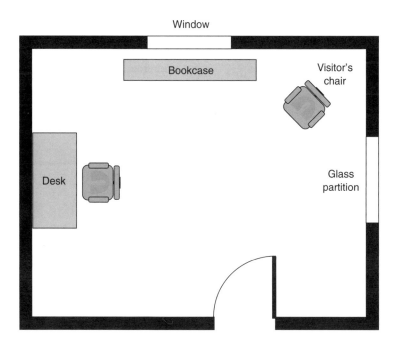

Certain objects strategically placed around the office can increase the status and power of the occupant. Massive desks, or a wall covered with photos, awards, or qualifications that the occupant has received, can intimidate others.

A supervisor who keeps an employee waiting a long time (more than 15 minutes), devotes only a short time to the meeting when a longer conference is appropriate, and meets only occasionally with the employee, is communicating a negative, disrespectful attitude toward that employee.

Physical barriers are not always necessary to convey the protection of personal space; people are always conscious of their intimate zone and its violations. The butler who does not listen to the conversations of guests, the pedestrian who avoids staring at an embracing couple, or the person who becomes preoccupied with a magazine during another's nearby telephone conversation all show some awareness of communication property rights. A person will adjust both his body language and proxemics to relay a message of phony disinterest.

Answers to *Meeting Manners* exercise

1. You should say the boss's name first. Proper introductions have a pecking order with the person of rank, honor, or importance mentioned first.
2. No
3. Your salad plate is to the left of the entrée plate. An easy way to remember this is to think of the BMW car. From left to right, think: Bread, Meal, Water. Bread and all food to the left of the plate are yours. Water and all drinks to the right are yours.
4. Yes
5. D
6. A, B, or C
7. Pushing back your plate is not the single indication that you are finished eating. Think of your plate as a clock. Put your fork and knife in the 10 and 4 o'clock positions with the utensils pointing at 10 o'clock and the base of the utensils at 4 o'clock. The knife should be on the outside with its blades facing inward towards the fork.
8. False. Businesses should be gender neutral.
9. B
10. B

Personal Selling Power: Basis for a Successful Meeting and a Victorious Close

13

Forget closing; it's about beginning a relationship or opening an account. Even if closing comes at the end of the selling cycle, it really signals the launch of a hopefully longstanding client relationship. Instead of labeling it as a final event, it should be about securing commitment, asking for the order, or getting the decision.

Visual closing first impressions

Clothing has the power to influence not only how others perceive a person, but how a person regards himself. When a person feels good about the way he looks, he feels better about himself. Considering the type of visual impression a salesperson makes at the closing is as important as his presentation.

Clients decide in a short amount of time whether a person is reliable, truthful, and professional. The salesperson's clothing, posture, and neatness are visible and brimming with clues about his background. Once a prospect draws conclusions about a negotiator's identity from his outward symbols, he acts accordingly. Visually creating a positive first impression and a positive final impression are as important as a person's words, tone of voice, and body language. Negotiators should:

1. Wear clean clothing that is appropriate for the occasion; check shoes.
2. Consider every aspect of appearance, from hair length for males to the amount of make-up worn by women.
3. Take bulky items out of the top jacket pockets. Too many pens, numerous pencils, bulky spectacle cases, and pocket calculators are signs of clutter.

4. Hire a good tailor for a great fit. Inappropriate clothing color, improper accessories, offensive ties, noisy jewelry, and tacky attaché cases can ruin an overall image.
5. Make certain that their hands are well groomed.
6. Sit and stand tall. Move with grace and assertion. Good posture and a confident stride indicate that a person is happy and proud.
7. Respect time. Be on time; respect the other person's schedules.

The fact that people form lasting impressions very quickly does not seem to detract from their strength and permanence. Simple mistakes in clothing choices or personal presentation should not obscure a person's natural gifts and talents for a successful close.

Use an effective waiting posture

Before the appointment, a salesperson will typically have to wait in a lobby, a reception area, or an assistant's office. It is imperative that the salesperson monitor his nonverbal behavior and facial expressions while he is deep in thought because office insiders are sure to notice. Efficient, observant receptionists are aware of a salesperson's waiting posture and typically make a mental note of it—either positive or negative.

1. Sit in a comfortable, composed posture.
2. Relax.
3. Use creative imagery, think positive thoughts.
4. Initiate a personal appearance inventory.
5. Look the part; act the part; think the part.
6. Avoid fidgeting and nervously scanning documents.
7. Keep in mind that negotiation depends on effective communication.
8. SMILE!

Full-body listening

Effective listening is a crucial, yet often overlooked, skill in business activities. Research indicates that adults spend 70 percent of their waking hours in verbal and listening communication. As a method of taking in information, we listen far more than we read and write. Full-body listening is not instinctive; it is a learned skill that involves the entire body: the eyes, the ears, the heart, and the mind.

Speaking rates for adults average between 125 to 145 words per minute; listening rates for adults average between 400 to 600 words per minute. Knowing these facts, one can readily understand why a person's mind wanders as he listens to a speaker. Concentration and self discipline are crucial to eliminating distractions. A committed listener knows that he has to understand the speaker's key points, overcome boredom, interpret voice inflection, recognize nonverbal clues, and comprehend the main message with all of his senses for true communication to occur.

listening vs. hearing

Hearing is simply taking in sounds; listening is making sense of the sounds that a person hears. It involves a sophisticated mental process and demands energy and discipline. Just as one can improve negotiating skills, he can also enhance listening skills. Since effective listening involves the entire body, it is easy to recognize that listening is an active, not a passive, process. A skilled listener accepts the perspective of the speaker and nonverbally acknowledges what he hears, all the while remaining nonjudgmental.

Since true communication occurs by developing a level of "commonness" between people, a competent listener knows his responsibility in the communication process. An accomplished listener understands that he cannot simply be present and expect to absorb what he hears; he knows that he has to take an active part in every facet of listening. Nonverbal acknowledgement—a basic, universal, human need—builds teamwork, trust, and a sense of belonging. Smiling, head nods, leaning in—all nonverbal gestures that convey a sense of respect to a speaker.

THREE LEVELS OF LISTENING

Madelyn Burley-Allen, author of *Listening: The Forgotten Skill*, (1995) lists three levels of listening. She reports that the three levels are not sharply distinct, but they are general categories into which people fall.

level 1: empathetic listening—At this level the listener shows both verbally and nonverbally that he is truly listening. These individuals refrain from judging the speaker and place themselves in the other person's position. Level 1 listeners do not allow for distractions and listen with understanding and empathy.

level 2: hearing words, but not really listening—Listeners at this level stay at the surface of the communication and typically do not understand the deeper meanings of the speaker's words. These highly logical individuals listen but have more concern with content than with feelings.

level 3: listening in spurts—This listener tunes in and out to the ongoing conversation. He tends to focus mainly on himself and his next chance to speak. At this level, the listener appears to be faking attention while thinking about unrelated matters, making judgments, and forming his rebuttal.

❶ull-body listening posture

The manner in which a person listens and encourages others will strongly influence how others respond to him. Effective listening encourages another person to continue talking, thus giving the negotiator additional information. Often effective listening depends on what is going on in the head and heart of those communicating. True message reading comes from understanding the attitudes and feelings inside the speaker.

The following full-body listening gestures help to convey interest to the listener.

1. Face the person with an open, relaxed posture.
2. Acknowledge the speaker by:
   ◉ nodding the head
   ◉ slightly tilting the head
   ◉ creating facial expressions that match the speaker's feelings
   ◉ making eye contact
3. Lean forward in the chair.
4. Avoid self-touching gestures that express uncertainty.
5. Steer clear of frowning.
6. Make meaningful notes.
7. Stay away from doodling, clock watching, and pencil tapping.
8. Ask questions for clarification.

❶ffensive body language

To conceal contempt, disapproval, or opposition at meeting proceedings, avoid the following body language:

◉ Yawning like a lion.
◉ Tapping one's pencil on the front of one's teeth.

- Slouching ironically low in one's chair and sticking one's feet straight out underneath the boardroom table.
- Sighing shamelessly.
- Thumbing one's BlackBerry when the CEO is speaking.
- Throwing things at other people, even in fun.
- Checking one's cellular telephone messages.
- Muttering blatantly "Give me a break" or "As if."

Closing a negotiation

Successful negotiating—an attempt by two people to achieve a mutually acceptable solution—should not result in a winner and a loser. It is a process that ends either with a satisfying conclusion for both sides or with failure for both sides. Hopefully, the conclusion of the negotiation is the beginning of a longstanding client relationship.

Before moving toward closure in a negotiation and putting things in writing, it is important to ensure that both parties clearly focus on the relevant issues. Are they talking about the same thing? Proper terminology used in the final agreement assures the clear and accurate recording of terms.

Closing requires confidence and passion that a product or service is worth more than the price that the seller is asking the prospect to pay. Top sales people consistently show two behavior characteristics that get them the sale: the capacity to be friendly (empathy opens the sale) and the ability to be firm (ego drive closes the sale).

Although every negotiator may have some of these attitudes, they must be applied in equal measure. Sales people who are too friendly will get along fine with the customer and will easily get a whole series of positive signals, but they may sometimes lack the inner strength to ask for the order. When a negotiator is too firm, on the other hand, he may bulldoze through a sale, annoy the prospect, and cause unnecessary changes from positive to negative signals.

The ability to be friendly and to create positive signals is only a means to an end—the sale, the satisfied need, the happy customer. To turn positive signals into dollars, a negotiator needs to balance his friendliness with his firmness to close the sale.

VISUAL, AUDITORY, AND ACTION CLOSES

People who want to close more sales simply need to STOP TALKING and let the client ask for a solution to a problem. The negotiator's job is not to dominate the conversation, but to listen and encourage the prospect to keep on talking. Research indicates that closing ratio increases as negotiator talking decreases.

Astute listening allows the negotiator to identify the type of language and information his client prefers to use and hear. If the negotiator has matched his vocabulary to his customer's, a successful close stressing these preferences will seem natural. When attempting to match the client's preferred language, a negotiator must realize that each person has his own meanings for words because he filters them through his past beliefs, knowledge, education, upbringing, and experiences. As a result, no two people have exactly the same meaning for the same word or expression; meanings are not in words, meanings are in people.

There are presently over 750,000 thousand words in the *Oxford English Dictionary*. Based on education level, the average person in the United States has a vocabulary of approximately 5,000 to 8,000 words. That is, he can understand 5,000 to 8,000 words, but he actually only uses an average of 1,200 words each day. It is interesting that each of those 1,200 words has between 20 and 25 meanings. That means that two people can use 1,200 words each with the possibility of 24,000 meanings. Thus it is extremely wise to constantly summarize the speaker's words during a conversation.

visual closes—These are the 'show and tell' types. Using pen and paper, the salesperson should demonstrate in black and white how the prospect will benefit from the purchase. A written summary of the pros and cons of his buying decision appeals to the visual buyer.

auditory closes—Prospects who prefer an auditory vocabulary and information are most likely to buy when the close involves decision-making statements or asking questions to which the only reasonable answer is "Yes." Constantly hearing himself verbally agree to statements has a powerful psychological impact on the auditory customer. Seasoned sales executives know the benefit of this phenomenon and obtain several "Yes" responses before they ask for the order.

The extra incentive close for the auditory buyer involves the salesperson making his offer sound irresistible by verbalizing it with excitement and enthusiasm in his voice. Verbally summarizing the product benefits leads the customer from a thinking mode to a decision mode and forces him to make a logical ruling.

action closes—The action-oriented prospect will display positive buying signals early in the sales presentation. He:

- ◉ Nods his head up and down.
- ◉ Makes physical contact with the salesperson.
- ◉ Rubs his hands together.
- ◉ Grabs a pen for writing.
- ◉ Walks around the product, touching it, adjusting it.

Oftentimes a customer may want to make the purchase but needs a gentle push to make the decision. The salesperson, on the other hand, knows that too much assertiveness could be counterproductive. When this happens, the salesperson should slowly begin packing up his sales literature, order forms and samples, leading the customer to believe that he is on his way out the door. If this maneuver is conducted properly, the prospect often lowers his defenses. The salesperson should then turn to the customer and refocus on the dominant buying motive. He should save a special finance offer, an extra incentive, or a new creative solution to the client's problem for the pack-up and leave close. Physically moving closer to the customer's door lowers the client's resistance and aids to a successful comeback and final close.

BASICS FOR A SUCCESSFUL CLOSE

Getting to a successful close means that the salesperson has managed his own and his client's body language effectively. For successful meeting conclusions:

- ◉ Never begin a close unless positive buying signals have been recorded.
- ◉ Continue to use open, encouraging signals and maintain good eye contact.
- ◉ Select a close that suits the client based on his preference for visual, auditory, or action words and information.
- ◉ Redirect the selling approach if the client signals doubt during the close—ask open questions, restate benefits, and continue to respond with positive, supportive signals.
- ◉ Smile and thank the client for the order.
- ◉ Reassure the buyer that the order is only the beginning of a long-term relationship.
- ◉ Schedule a follow-up call to check on how the client's purchase has improved his business operation or personal situation.

the rules of nonverbal selling power

David Lewis, in his book *The Secret Language of Success: Using Body Language to Get What You Want* (1989), suggests some of the following rules for successful selling experiences.

First Meetings

RULE 1:   Manage every second of a first meeting. Positive first impressions are a necessity.

RULE 2:   Always initiate and respond to the eyebrow flash (emits friendliness, approval, or agreement).

RULE 3:   Break eye contact downward. Perplexing upward eye breaks convey a lack of interest in the other person.

RULE 4:   Never hold a gaze for more than three seconds when first meeting someone. Look; then break eye contact briefly. Disobeying this rule can produce a negative impression.

RULE 5:   Use the smile most suitable to the situation. Inappropriate smiles can create as negative an impression as not smiling at all.

Using Space—While Standing

RULE 6:   Never invade another person's intimate zone unintentionally.

RULE 7:   Take into account and respect individual and cultural spatial differences.

RULE 8:   Never stand directly opposite an unknown male or adjacent to an unfamiliar female. Men prefer to start a conversation at a more side-on position and gradually work their way around to a more frontal one. Women prefer to begin encounters at a frontal position.

RULE 9:   Never stand when someone else is sitting. It suggests a desire to dominate or intimidate the other person.

RULE 10:   Avoid sitting in low, deep arm chairs. Confidence and power are difficult to convey while sitting far back in a chair.

While Shaking Hands

RULE 11:   Apply a moderate amount of pressure when shaking hands. Limit the handshake to three pumps and attempt to hold the handshake for approximately six seconds.

RULE 12:   Communicate dominance by using the palm-down handshake. To express friendship and a desire for cooperation, use the vertical handshake. To convey submission, employ the palm-up handshake.

RULE 13:   Stay away from wearing tinted, dark, or reflecting glasses to avoid appearing dishonest or shady.

RULE 14:   Use a head tilt, direct eye contact, and a warm smile to increase warmth and impact when first meeting someone or when asking for help or cooperation.

RULE 15:   Avoid reading from a script when addressing a group. Either memorize the presentation or use brief notes. Scan the room and encourage listening by making eye contact with each meeting attendee.

Power Plays

RULE 16:   Walk slowly, walk deliberately, and walk tall. Take the time to review the surroundings. Hurried walkers appear disorganized.

RULE 17:   Select a chair that is easy to get in and out of and is at the same height level as the negotiating partner's chair.

RULE 18:   Stick to the 15-minute rule for being kept waiting. Call a halt to the intended meeting unless there is an obviously valid and genuine reason for the 15-minute delay.

Reading Others

RULE 19:   Detect anxiety in another person by looking at his feet and his hands rather than his face. Watch for his body language 'leakage' gestures, as these small subconscious, controlled movements relieve his inner tensions.

RULE 20:   Watch for key buying silent signals: a sudden release of tension (sigh), intensified eye contact, greater proximity, and increased chin stroking (evaluation).

RULE 21:   Scrutinize for increased self-touching deception gestures that involve rubbing or stroking the ears, nose, or eyes. Too few gestures or aggressive, forced movements of the feet, hands, or mouth are predictors of dishonesty.

Constant improvement in closing sales

Every sales interview affords the opportunity for the sales executive to improve his selling effectiveness. However, most people do not review every sales interview and therefore continue to repeatedly make the same mistakes. Searching constantly for the positive and the negative in each encounter allows the sales executive to improve.

An individual who wants to become a 90 percent closer makes certain that he reviews every sales interview immediately after the sales encounter. In his car, at a restaurant, or in a conference room back at the office, he finds ways to improve. Asking himself what he did well, what needs improvement for next time, what surprises were there, and what will he do differently next time allows him to make the proper adjustments in his selling techniques. Every sales encounter should end with a commitment to change what did not work and to enhance what worked well.

Exercise

Study each picture sequence that follows to determine the intended body language gesture of individual meeting attendees.

1. Who is being the most disrespectful?
2. Which man is locked in his opinion?
3. Who shows the most disapproval and disinterest?
4. Who is the most defensive of the three? What gestures show this?
5. What lack-of-concern gesture is visible in this setting?

1. What four open and honesty gestures are apparent from the individual on the left?
2. What two defensive gestures is the woman using?
3. Identify the confident or superior gesture in the picture.
4. Who is using the critical evaluation gesture?
5. Who is the most argumentative and why?

Bibliography

Axtell, R. E. (1998). *Gestures.* New York: John Wiley & Sons, Inc.

Beier, E. G., and Valens, E. G. (1992). *People reading.* Maryland: Scarborough House.

Birdwhistell, R. (1952). *Introduction to kinesics.* Louisville, KY: University of Louisville Press.

Birdwhistell, R. (1970). *Kinesics and context.* Pennsylvania: University of Pennsylvania Press.

Burley-Allen, M. (1995). *Listening: The forgotten skill.* New York: John Wiley & Sons, Inc.

Carnegie, D. (1937). *How to win friends and influence people.* New York: Simon and Schuster.

Darwin, Charles. (1872). *The expression of emotion in man and animals.* New York: Appleton-Century-Crofts.

Dimitrius, J. (1998). *Reading people.* New York: Random House, Inc.

Dimitrius, J., & Mazzarella, M. (2000). *Put your best foot forward.* New York: Simon and Schuster.

Dunkell, S. (1978). *Sleep positions.* New York: New American Library, New York.

Ekman, P. (1973). *Darwin and facial expressions.* New York: Academic Press.

———. Ekman, P. (1992). *Telling lies.* New York: W. W. Norton & Company.

Ekman, P., & Friesen, W. (1975). *Unmasking the face.* New Jersey: Prentice-Hall.

Ekman, P., Friesen, W., & Ellsworth, P. (1972). *Emotion of the human face.* New York: Pergamon Press.

Fast, J. (1970). *Body language.* New York: Simon and Schuster.

———. (1991). *Subtext.* New York: Viking Publishers.

Glass, L. (1993). *He says, she says.* New York: Putnam Publishing Group.

Goldman, D. (1985). *Vital lies, simple truths*. New York: Simon and Schuster.

Gschwandtner, G. (1985). *Nonverbal selling power.* New Jersey: Prentice Hall, Inc..

Hargrave, J. (1995). *Let me see your body talk.* Dubuque, IA: Kendall/Hunt Publishing Company.

Hargrave, J., & Weiser, A. (2000). *Judge the jury.* Dubuque, IA: Kendall/Hunt Publishing Company.

Hindle, T. (1998). *Negotiating skills.* New York: DK Publishing, Inc.

Kuei, C. A. (1998). *Face reading.* London: Souvenir Press Ltd.

Lewis, D. (1989). *The secret language of success.* New York: Carroll & Graff Publishers, Inc.

McKay, M., Davis, M., & Fanning, P. (1995). *Messages.* California: New Harbor Publications.

Mehrabian, A. (1971). *Silent messages.* Belmont, CA: Wadsworth.

———. (1969). *Tactics of social influence.* New Jersey: Prentice-Hall.

Morris, D. (1994). *Body talk.* New York: Crown Publishers, Inc.

Morris, D. (1971). *Intimate behavior.* London: Cape, London.

Morris, D. (1977). *Manwatching.* New York: Abrams.

Morris, D. (1968). *The naked ape.* New York: McGraw-Hill.

Morrison, T., Conaway, W. A., & and Borden, G. A. (1994). *Kiss, bow, or shake hands.* Avon, MA: Adams Media Corporation.

Nierenberg, G. I. (1973). *Fundamentals of negotiating.* New York: Hawthorn/Dutton.

Nierrenberg, G., & Calero, H. (1971). *How to read a person like a book.* New York: Hawthorn Books.

Pease, A. (1984). *Signals.* Canada: Bantam Books, Inc.

Quilliam, S. (2004). *Body language.* Buffalo, NY: Firefly Books.

Tannen, D. (1994). *Talking from 9 to 5.* New York: William Morrow and Company.

———. (1990). *You just don't understand.* New York: Ballantine Books, New York.

Wainwright, G. R. (1993). *Body language.* Chicago, IL: NTC Publishing Group.